Growing up in Saldanha Bay on the West Coast kindled in JOHAN BAKKES a lifelong love of nature, travel and adventure. As an eight-year-old he joined students of the Military Academy on "Vasbyt" in the Cedarberg.

After his schooldays at Afrikaans Hoër Seunskool an HSRC survey of the best-paid professions resulted in the part-time Tukkies student opting for a career as a chartered accountant.

Two opposing principles – standard of living versus quality of life – led to doubts about the merits of an eighteen-hour workday and after he had completed his military service, early retirement without financial backing became a serious consideration.

The ideal was to be a professionally qualified bum. However, two children and an exaggerated sense of responsibility put paid to any possibility of hitting the road. He became a professor, instructing students at UNISA in the finer points of accounting.

With more time at his disposal, he established the safari enterprise Induku, venturing into Africa with backpack and 4x4. Moreover, whether as logistics organiser or mere participant, he undertook several death-defying expeditions covered by the media. All in the name of travel and adventure.

And now? Presently he is on the academic staff of the University of the Western Cape and lives somewhere in Paarl.

He is still on the move.

C. JOHAN BAKKES

to HELL and gone

TRANSLATED BY ELSA SILKE

Human & Rousseau
Cape Town   Pretoria

Human & Rousseau
an imprint of NB Publishers
40 Heerengracht, Cape Town 8001
www.humanrousseau.com
© 2008 Johan Bakkes

Translated by Elsa Silke
Design by Susan Bloemhof
Printed and bound by Paarl Print,
Oosterland Street, Paarl, South Africa

First edition, first printing 2008

ISBN-10: 0-7981-4944-2
ISBN-13: 978-0-7981-4944-0

For all my fellow travellers.
And for my children, who have to continue with the journey.

If you don't know, you won't understand, and if you had known, you wouldn't have asked.
– Anon

Contents

The day the world laughed   11
Hell on earth   15
Promotion   21
Uhuru   25
The skirmish   31
And I told him   35
The kukri   38
My brother's keeper   42
Angel   45
Calculate the cost   49
A different kind of Christmas   54
The apricot lady of Nouadhibou   58
Beautiful   63
Justice always prevails   67
Landmine   71
Sangoma   75
A lucky man   79
A father   82
The women of Skardu   85
The world was sleeping . . .   90
Wealth   94
Flotsam   98
Bread on the water   101
It's late, but my future is beckoning   106
Our land   110
Sekkab Annan   114
The plan   118
On the wings of Bonnies   122

A view of Everest   125
Mignon's forest   129
Der Reiter von Eros   132
Gert Geloof   137
Half-man   140
Purgatory   146
A moer of a party at an empty graveside   150
Ambassador   153
A man must have papers   158
Judging a book by its cover   162
Headstrong   167
African roads   172
Where the hell is Mombolo?   175
The professor and the pin-up girl   180
Heavy as lead   187
All in the mind   190
Barry Viljoen   194
Trapezium   198
Love   203
Saints   206
For the sake of . . .   211
Reunion   215
Dr Jan van Elfen   218
Dreams and realities   223
This is where I draw the line   292
An after-story   297

Glossary   299
Acknowledgements   303

The day the world laughed

"That woman in the dress and bracelets is my dad!" I heard my six-year-old son protest indignantly on the other side of the supermarket shelves. When I joined him, pushing my loaded trolley, he explained: "Pa, those people are looking at you and talking behind your back!"

My appearance has always drawn a second glance from strangers and has been a thorn in the flesh of my loved ones, since they could not choose me.

It's difficult to describe myself. My mother likes to say: "He's not exactly an oil painting."

I was her first attempt – the other three didn't turn out too badly.

Mother-in-law says: "If only the man would have a haircut and trim his beard a little!"

The dominee has been heard to say: "It's not right for a deacon to wear bangles up to his armpits. The members of the congregation are liable to miss the collection plate."

My wife says: "Why do you have to be so sloppy? Surely you're not thinking of going shopping barefoot and in a kikoi?"

Babies scream and grab their mothers' breasts if I coo anywhere near them. Women give me a wide berth and teenagers exclaim in loud voices: "Hey, did you check that oke?"

Perhaps there's a bit of wilfulness involved, because I *have*, on occasion, worn a tie or something black for a grand event. On the whole, however, I expect people to accept me the way I feel comfortable.

The only place where no one cares about my appearance is in the bush. Naturally I don't care either, especially as my only use for water is to dilute whisky. That's why I'm at my best in the bush.

Besides, there's no time for frills in the veld.

Covered in six weeks' dirt, we lay in all-round defence somewhere in Angola. Hiding behind a bush on the Kwando flood plain in the Caprivi, you fervently hope that the bloody elephant, no more than three metres away, won't smell you. Or it'll be tickets.

When you wake on the banks of the Zambezi in Zimbabwe to find a lioness peering inquisitively into your face, you suspect it's your breath and not your scream that sends her scampering off.

In the Mana Pools reserve an elephant once stepped over me without touching me, as I lay on the ground pretending to be a log. I remember the front and rear trunks dangling in front of my face. I was thankful that I hadn't used a deodorant for days.

Any chance meeting with people, however, is sure to result in open-mouthed astonishment and an undignified hee-hee.

Chipata in Zambia: youngsters crowding around me. "Jambo," I greet them. Pointing at my bandana and long knife, they retort: "Rambo?"

That earned me a nickname among my fellow travellers – Sylvester Alone.

Nouakchott, Mauritania: Islamic children staring at me, as I sat leaning with my back against the wall of a mud hut, exhausted. Until their mother shooed them away in Arabic and apologised to me in English.

At the hotel in Katmandu we were enjoying a few beers in the garden when the staff began to file past, staring and greeting. It was only when the manager came over to inquire whether the one with the tousled beard happened to be a WWF wrestler – "the Undertaker" or some such person – that I understood what the fuss was about.

Also in Nepal, we were heading for the Himalayan glaciers. Off into the mountains, blissfully removed from grinning onlookers. The only live creatures, apart from our Sherpa guides, would be yaks and isolated Buddhist monks in cliff-hanging monasteries and abbeys.

When we weren't thickly padded against cold of minus 20 degrees, I was most comfortable in my desert garb – Arab robe, headdress and staff.

Our trip was coming to an end. During the descent to Junbesi, a village on the Everest route, our guide took us to the Thubten

Choling abbey and cloister, home to 400 Buddhist monks and nuns.

Here they isolate themselves from the outside world and study philosophy and ethics. They are serious people. They aspire to attain Nirvana. Their daily ritual includes hours of reading page upon page out of prayer books.

We had not bathed for eleven days. We took off our boots. Respectfully our guides led us into the prayer hall. The candlelight was dim. Incense was burning and gold statues of Buddha stood everywhere. It sounded like a beehive as a few hundred monks softly murmured their prayers. Dressed in orange or red togas, they were all sitting in the same position – cross-legged, their bald heads bowed. Occasionally someone turned a page in his rectangular prayer booklet. "Hummmmm-hummmmm."

Their lives are spent in complete isolation, with no contact with their fellow man. Amazed, we looked at this extraordinary sight.

As he was turning the page, a monk gave me a sidelong glance. What he beheld was a figure from another Bible – a savage with long hair and beard, two kilograms of copper bracelets encircling his arms, a long staff, a white robe and red mountaineering socks.

Between the humming he started to "Hee hee hee," checked himself and resorted again to "Hummmmm-hummmmm" . . . until, "Hee hee hee," it came again from the lowered head. Suddenly everybody was looking up and soon the entire hall was going "Hee hee hee" at the sight of John the Baptist standing there in the flesh.

At that very moment – to hell 'n gone at the back of beyond – I realised that my children's greatest fear had become a reality.

The whole world was laughing.

Hell on earth

"This is becoming a dangerous situation," muttered Brook Kassa, giving me an anxious look. He tried to start the Land Cruiser, but nothing happened.

It was like something from a nightmare or a Freddy Krueger movie. The vehicle was surrounded by a milling, pushing, grinning, gesticulating, shouting horde. Aggression flashed from their sharpened teeth and they waved their AK47s wildly. They were the Afar people from hell on earth . . .

Hell on earth? The expression means different things to different people. To some it's in their job, their relationships, or a loss they have suffered. By the grace of God I went in search of mine physically.

It started years ago. My search for those "different" places, where few people care to go. The adventure, the moment itself and returning to tell the tale.

In 1999 my daughter and I stood on top of Kilimanjaro, the highest point on our continent. Where is the lowest point? I suddenly wondered as I stood gasping for air.

Bits of information were subsequently gathered here and there. The answer was the Danakil desert – in the north of Ethiopia, bordering on Eritrea and Djibouti.

Not much information is available on the Danakil. Documents that were found described it as:

"The most inhospitable place on earth."

"The warmest place on earth inhabited by man."

"The lowest dryland on earth."

But no detailed description of how, where and what. Travel guides on Ethiopia and Eritrea barely mention the area. Nowhere could I find directions for the journey to hell on earth.

That was enough for my friend Kalie Kirsten, wine farmer on the outskirts of Stellenbosch, and me. We wanted to go there, to visit Ethiopia, its churches, its castles and the Lost Ark of the Covenant as well.

But no one in Ethiopia was willing to go to hell!

"We will take you to the edge of the Danakil, the Afar will

16

take you further – hope you enjoy it," was the best any tour guide was willing to do. And the two of us, accompanied by Roland Berry, an ophthalmologist, and Paul Andrag, another wine farmer, set off for Ethiopia . . .

"We cannot go further, the salt crust will break and the vehicle will disappear." I looked at my friends despondently. It was 40 degrees Celsius and we were 120 metres below sea level – about five kilometres away there was a dark spot on the pan: the salt mines of the Danakil . . .

With Brook Kassa, our Asmara guide from Addis Ababa, behind the wheel, we had left the Ethiopian highlands at Angula. During the descent down the escarpment we encountered camel caravans carrying blocks of salt to Mekele. The salt mines were our destination. To my knowledge, this is one of the few caravan routes of the ancient world that still exist. The ivory, silk, spice and slave routes lapsed into disuse a long time ago. How long these salt caravans will still continue, is an open question. It's a lifestyle for the Afar, the people of the Danakil. It's hard to believe that it can be economical. A block of salt is sold for 10 birr (about R10) at the market in Mekele. A young, strong camel can carry 16 blocks – the journey to the market and back takes eight days.

The Afar is a proud nation, extremely jealous of this piece of desert. Outsiders are regarded with suspicion. The Habushas (the collective name for other Ethiopians) deem it reckless to travel through Afar territory. Sir Wilfred Thesiger, the first Westerner to traverse the Danakil as late as 1934, wrote: "The Afar invariably castrated any man or boy whom they killed, removing both the penis and scrotum – an obvious trophy – and obtaining it gave the additional satisfaction of dishonouring the corpse . . ."

At Berhale we made a stop. It is a godforsaken, windswept settlement on the banks of a broad, dry river bed. It was sweltering, and people took refuge in hessian dwellings. The most beautiful girls peered around the corners. We photographed them secretly.

17

If we wanted to continue, we would have to take along an Afar representative. We already had an envoy from the Tigre tourist bureau in Mekele in the vehicle. The provincial government wouldn't allow us into the Danakil without a monitor. The Cruiser was packed to the brim as we made our way down a dry tributary.

We were no longer driving on a road, but over boulders and river stones. Brook had grown pale beside me. The deeper we went down the dongas and ravines, the more I realised the risk we were taking. No one should venture down here in one vehicle only. A mechanical breakdown could result in death. As Brook came to understand his error in judgment, he developed the runs and kept disappearing behind a rock.

Then the mountains opened up and we burst out on a basalt plain. The wind gusted and warm dust poured in everywhere. These were truly the gates of hell. Suddenly we saw a small gazelle in the distance. It was the Penzeln gazelle. It is found only in the Danakil, and I realised how privileged I was to be one of the few travellers ever to see this rare antelope in the flesh.

We were thoroughly fed up with bouncing and jostling, so in the late afternoon we made Brook stop. We pitched a windswept camp beside a small, warm stream. We submerged our cool drinks, water and beer in the tepid water. While the Askaris were preparing our meal, we lay in the water, ruminating about the day.

Late that night, with mosquitoes and desert bugs of uncertain origin chewing at us, a camel caravan silently joined our camp.

We loaded our equipment. It was only a few more kilometres to sea level. It was not light yet, but we were already pouring with sweat. There was an apprehensive excitement in the air. When we hit "ground zero" according to the GPS, we cheered uproariously.

Then, as far as the eye could see, there was a pan. Makgadikgadi, my arse – it extended almost to the Red Sea. Apparently it's the remainder of a large inland sea that has evaporated. It was once part of the Red Sea but was isolated by volcanic eruptions about 10 000 years ago.

We stopped at Arho, a small settlement at the edge of the rift valley. It is the hottest place on earth inhabited by humans. The salt miners from hell.

The Afar glared at us suspiciously. The man from Berhale explained why we were there and handed out quat – a narcotic leaf chewed by the Ethiopians. We negotiated for the camping equipment to be left there, thus making the vehicle lighter for the trip across the salt flats. If we broke through the crust, our vehicle, and we along with it, would disappear for ever . . .

We had progressed about two kilometres across the pan when the realisation dawned – we could go no further!

Will we have to turn around? I wondered, staring despondently at the dark patch on the distant horizon. The sun was hot and white.

"I'm walking," I said and grabbed a water bottle.

And so we set off. It soon became a struggle through salt and water. It grew hotter and hotter. The glare of the sun was blinding. Like an automaton I continued, my eyes fixed on the dark patch up ahead.

After a while I became aware of a strange noise, almost like the sound of the seals at Cape Cross, and I realised it was the bellowing and moaning of a multitude of camels. The mine was within reach and we pushed on with renewed effort. The water was growing considerably warmer . . .

And then I walked into another world. It was almost unreal. As if I found myself in a scene from the *Star Wars* underworld, or a medieval nightmare. In the stifling air, amid more than two thousand camels, wild men with sharpened teeth, dressed in tattered clothing, were carving blocks of salt out of the earth's crust with antiquated tools. There was hustle and bustle and shouting and bellowing. The glaring sun, the mirages and the heat lent to the scene an aura of science fiction.

The envoy from Mekele explained that the miners arrived at

19

the mine from Arho with their camels in the morning, when it was still dark; at night, when it was slightly cooler, they returned with the yield of the day on their camels' backs.

We took photographs.

Before long the Afar guide began to gesticulate uneasily. He pointed up and then down. We didn't really understand, but he began to walk back in the direction of our vehicle, invisible in the distance somewhere near the edge of the pan. It was a distance of about five or six kilometres. Halfway there I realised the danger! The increased temperature of the salt water was almost unbearable. When my sandals were sucked into the salt, I could literally feel my feet boiling. It became a mad rush to escape from the jaws of the devil.

With every suction, my feet were scorching. The last twenty metres were pure hell. We realised if we had left the mine half an hour later, we would have been burned to death on this pan one by one . . .

"This is becoming a dangerous situation," muttered Brook Kassa as the Afar of Arho crowded round the vehicle. They refused to let us go. What had we come here for? Who were we to want to escape from the underworld? If your road takes you to hell, and the angels of darkness get their hands on you, you can't just presume that you will be allowed to return!

And then the engine fired, and with a roar we burst through the milling mass – back to the light.

Promotion

As I was dragging my backpack through the thick sand in sweltering heat, I thought: Please remind me what the hell I am doing here!

Sweat was soaking through my bandana and trickling into my beard. My brain had shut down, so that I no longer saw the shiny rippling of the river to my right and the rough cliffs surrounding the canyon. People were trudging behind me. My clients and my responsibility.

Philemon – or Fielies, as I had named him – was Ndbele. Born in the Messina district, he had found work in Pretoria as driver and apprentice mechanic. Those two towns comprised his entire world and frame of reference. When I had picked him up that morning, I saw that his eyes were glistening with excitement. We were on our way to recover a bakkie of mine that had broken down in distant Namibia. He was apprehensive, but with his brand-new, first-ever passport and his "baas" – boss – by his side he was ready for adventure. To Fielies "baas" was not the way an inferior person addressed his superior – it was my title, my name. "Meneer" or "Johan" simply didn't carry the same weight.

For the past fifteen years – year in, year out – I had been taking groups of people through the Fish River canyon in southern Namibia. It is a remarkable place that can only be appreciated the hard way and under one's own steam. Nowhere else in the world is the sky as blue. Nowhere else are the stars as bright. Nowhere else is the brilliance of the setting sun so bloody amazing. The eerie streaks of moonlight on the rough cliffs conjure up dreams of medieval castles and knights on horseback. Ever since my first visit I had felt the urge to make this harsh beauty accessible to others. I couldn't keep it to myself, I had argued.

En route Fielies and I chatted. When we passed through Ventersdorp I told him about the right-wing organisations; he told me about paying eight head of cattle and R10 000 as lobola. At Vryburg I showed him the place where the British hanged four colonialists for helping the Boers; he told me tales, passed on from one generation to the next, of Makapansgat in his district.

Fielies drank in everything I told him. It was as if new worlds were opening for him the further we travelled. The mealie fields of the Western Transvaal filled him with awe. He was amazed by the red dunes of the Kalahari. The great Gariep was the largest stretch of water he had ever seen. We had a beer at a little bar in Upington and looked out over the brown mass of water rushing past. Ill at ease in the unaccustomed luxury, he kept questioning me about this and that.

In the course of fifteen years the way I introduced visitors to the canyon and conducted the hiking tour had developed into a fine art. My main aim was to get every member of the large group safely to the other side and to establish coherence within the group. Equally important, though, was that everyone should enjoy the experience. My greatest reward was when, beer in hand, I watched the hikers arrive at the finish and saw the delight in their eyes.

It was late at night when we approached Karasburg. Crossing the border had been an adventure for Fielies. Proudly he had handed over his new passport to receive his first stamp. He was entering a foreign country for the first time.

I decided to book us into the hotel. "Fielies, I think you should call me 'meneer' around here," I suggested. Fielies gave me a strange look. We were allocated our rooms and I bought him a beer. The little bar was staunchly Afrikaans, as were the few cronies. Fielies went to his room and came back wide-eyed. "Baas, there's a shower – do you think I could wash?" I realised that even the stay in the hotel was a brand-new experience for him.

On a desert hike I wear my Arab robe, staff and headgear. Hence the nickname Moses among the Witbois of those parts. Mind you, on a previous occasion I had been promoted: A few members of my group had been unable to tackle the entire route and they were going to set out from Ai-Ais to join up with us. Because I thought they might not find the rendezvous, I sent ahead a Dutchman who had attached himself to our group. He greeted the others with the words: "Jesus is waiting for you."

But fifteen years is a long time and people are strange. I don't know whether it was my fault or theirs, but the joy was no longer there. Perhaps people were expecting me to make it worth their while, perhaps they came only for the party and failed to notice the beauty. That was when I decided: I was no longer going to take people to the canyon. I was going to put a stop to it. To add insult to injury, my bakkie broke down, and now Fielies and I were on our way to fetch it at Ai-Ais.

It was early when Fielies woke me with a cup of coffee. "Come, baas, let's go. I want to take a look at our bakkie." We drove through the granite hills leading up to the Fish River. As you approach the canyon, there is nothing to warn you that you are about to come across a vast chasm ripped into the earth. No one fails to be moved by the sight, but Fielies reacted with silent shock. I took him to the start of the hiking trail, where a few hikers had gathered, and sent him down the cliffs for a taste.

Beer in hand, I waited for his return, while I chatted to the group that was about to go down. Then he was back.

"Fielies, so what can you say to the meneer?" I emphasised "meneer" to remind Fielies of the presence of others.

"Meneer, my arse, baas," he replied, tears rolling down his cheeks. And I realised that there were still people to whom I wanted to show this place after all.

Uhuru

Were these drops of blood on the snow and ice in front of me? The steamed-up dark glasses were deceptive, for here and there I saw patches of green grass dancing in front of my eyes. The small cracks in the ice looked like bottomless crevasses as I forged ahead like an automaton. One, two, three shuffling steps; rest for ten counts. I no longer remembered why I was here.

"Is someone bleeding?" I croaked. "I think it's red cool drink," came a voice from above. I didn't look up. I could just see the tips of Cara's boots stepping in her father's tracks. "How are you, Pa?" my fourteen-year-old asked with shuddering breath. I really couldn't say, although I wished I could.

This particular piece of hell, consisting of ice, stone and inadequate air to breathe, had begun that morning at a quarter past midnight. Our guide had woken us with the words: "It's time; now is the hour." We had gone to bed with our boots on, insulated against cold of minus 15 degrees. Wearing a woollen cap, scarf and headlight, I had tumbled out of the igloo tent, looking like a yeti. Cara's words – "I've been dreading this moment" – had summed up my own feelings.

The route led up sheer cliffs that had been towering above us since the previous afternoon. This route had not been part of our initial planning. Our chief guide, Sammie, who had been studying our group of twenty-five over the previous four days, had recommended it and we had agreed, because by following this route – although fearfully steep – the group would be less liable to contract the dreaded altitude sickness.

Step by step, with Sammie in the lead and his assistant, Dixon, bringing up the rear, the train of headlights moved upward in the dark. After a mere twenty metres, Cara sank to her knees and vomited on the scree of the mountainside. I hastened to her side, but my heart sank into my boots. Either we turned round now or the opportunity was lost, and my eldest, with her fear of heights, would be forced to show her mettle. I pulled off my gloves and with gradually freezing fingertips I pushed an anti-nausea tablet down her throat and made her wash it down with a few sips of water. "My darling, today you'll be facing the most difficult time by far of your short life. You'll have to hang on," I urged.

We moved to the back, where Dixon encouraged Cara in broken English, interspersed with Swahili. She didn't say a word as we followed the vanishing climbers. Now it was only the Askari, my daughter and I making our way upward step by step over loose gravel and stones. Our words of encouragement were few and far between because, aside from the lack of oxygen, talking wasted energy. We were now more than 5 000 metres above sea level. We rested frequently, but only for short periods, or we ran the risk of freezing. When we stopped, Dixon held Cara in his arms, rubbed her back and crooned softly in her ear. The rubbing was alternated with gentle slapping to keep her awake. A lack of oxygen leads to drowsiness, followed by sleep, and ultimately death. My fatherly duties had been completely taken over by a stranger and I was bringing up the rear now. After patting her briefly on the shoulder, I had leaned on my walking stick and promptly fallen asleep, so that I'd had to force myself to wake up.

Time had lost all meaning. The need to keep climbing was predominant. Toes like ice cubes and numb hands made crawling on all fours nearly unbearable. In the light of the half-moon I was aware of vertical cliffs and yawning chasms on either side. Haltingly I warned Carla to look straight ahead and hold on for dear life. She might be the one who feared heights, but my fear for her safety struck terror in me. With my body I tried to shield her physically against the heights. She didn't say a word; just kept moving steadily along.

After a gruelling seven hours the dawn began to break. We were climbing up the western slope of the mountain and we realised that the sun would not reach us before we got to the ice field at the top. Only when it became lighter did we really understand how dangerous the climb had been up till that point. We were perched on the cliff like swallows, so high that we could no longer make out the base camp below. I would certainly not have

27

scaled those heights in daylight, especially not without equipment and ropes. It was nothing like the books, brochures and posters had said.

My road to Kilimanjaro had begun about 5 000 kilometres to the south a year before. One evening four of us on an eight-day hike through the Naukluft mountains had made a rash decision: "Let's climb that koppie."

Twenty-five souls were assembled and, with the dollar kicking the rand's arse, an operator was contacted in Tanzania. We had all hiked before so we decided, of the two well-known routes up the mountain, we wanted to do the Machame route. The Marangu route, the so-called Coca-Cola route, sounded too easy and impersonal.

With this intention, we were dropped off by Air Tanzania at the Kilimanjaro International Airport between Moshi and Arusha.That was where we met Sammie, his four guides, two chefs and forty bearers. The next day, with a drizzle in the air, we tackled the mountain.

On the first day we trudged up the mountainside through thick sludge and rain forests, with colobus monkeys chattering in the tall jungle trees, watching the antics of their descendants. It was also the last time we were clean. A late start saw the stragglers stumbling into camp at nine o'clock that night after an 18-kilometre struggle.

The next day we ascended steeply to a height of 3 800 metres. We reached the Shira camp at around three o'clock in the afternoon. Rain forest had made way for a lava plateau, but also for ice-cold mountain winds. The bearers pitched our tents and immediately began to prepare food on open fires. Tanzanian Askaris put all other climbers to shame. Carrying loads of up to 40 kilograms, they stride effortlessly up the slopes.

It was here at Shira that Sammie proposed the alternative route up the western slope, starting from the Arrow glacier. His plan entailed two more days of gradual ascent and acclimatisation, then a steep climb to the brim of Kilimanjaro before ascending to the highest point. His reasoning was sound and our leadership element consented. Little did we know . . .

A morning's hike through lava rock and alpine vegetation brought us to the foot of the Kibo massif. The altitude began to take its toll. Nausea, shortness of breath and headaches were the order of the day. The afternoon was passed taking in oxygen as we were too weak to do anything else. Sammie and his group tramped to and fro tirelessly, carrying water and wood, and even in those adverse conditions they served up a delicious supper of pasta, chicken and fresh vegetables. The cold drove us to our tents early.

We acclimatised until lunchtime the next day and, leaving the Lava Tower, we began an ascent of about 200 metres to the dilapidated hut at the foot of the Arrow glacier. The hut had been destroyed by a rock slide a few years before. It was there among the fallen boulders that Sammy had woken us that morning . . .

In single file we plodded along laboriously. The brink of Kibo was beckoning. Ice spilled over its side like icing sugar. As I pushed myself over the rim, the blinding sunlight on the snow made me reel. Dead tired, overwhelmed by dizziness and completely disoriented, I gasped for breath that wasn't there. A sip from my water bottle produced only ice. Fear of snow blindness made me put on my cracked Second World War desert shades, but they fogged up immediately. This added to the unreal aspect of the plateau that we had just set foot on. Sammie pointed out an ice-covered "Karoo koppie" some distance away. "Uhuru – two hours." The highest point in all of Africa, 200 metres higher than where I was standing now. Despondency got the better of a fellow climber. "I'm not going up there – I can't go on. I'm on top of Kilimanjaro now – why would I want to climb to its highest point?" I shared his sentiments, but stumbled on in the direction of the koppie – in part, at least, to stop Cara from slipping and plunging over the precipice.

Were those drops of blood on the ice and snow in front of me? An automated shuffling gait: rest, shuffle, rest. Ice crunching, breath rasping, vision clouding. The only way was up. Sammie was standing in front of me, fists in the air. Uhuru – freedom! I grabbed my daughter . . . my voice croaked even more. I was on the roof of my continent. My friends arrived: stumbling, crawling, crying, but our joy was boundless. Embraces, congratulations, photos, laughter – we had made it!

I sat down on a chunk of ice, lit a cigar and sipped some Hanepoot from the distant Cape – one doesn't die that easily after all.

The skirmish

How does one count crocodiles? "At night, on a boat, with a shooting lamp – you count the eyes and divide by two." Or so I was told.

"We're looking for someone to handle the logistics and the cooking for a South African delegation undertaking a census of the Nile crocodiles in the Luangwa River in cooperation with the Zambians."

A convoy of twenty-five vehicles, rubberducks and ski boats and sixty men arrived at the Kariba border post in Zimbabwe. Though the Zambian border posts had recently been opened to South Africans, an influx of this magnitude had not been anticipated by the bureaucrats. Frantic calls were made to Lusaka.

Of the original logistics group of seven only two had remained: my friend Ferdi and I. The wives of the others had decided it was far safer for them at home. Ferdi drove the supply truck and I cooked. It was hard work. We had been on the road for three days and everything had to happen in transit. Sixty men get hungry and two meals a day were mandatory.

Our little logistics team had established its own rhythm by now. In the late afternoon we moved ahead, found a suitable camp site at the roadside and unpacked our paraphernalia. Ferdi helped with food preparation and hit the sack. A long day's driving lay ahead the next day. I served the food, washed the dishes, prepared breakfast and food parcels and packed up everything. It usually took me all night. At first light we served breakfast and loaded the truck. As soon as Ferdi took up his position behind the wheel, I poured six fingers of rum over a three-day-old, fermented lemon half in a beer mug, added two Cal-C-Vita effervescent tablets, topped up the concoction with water and downed it. It knocked me out until lunchtime. I slept like a dead man, knowing that, as long as the good Lord kept our old charger on its wheels, Ferdi would keep it in the road.

It was late afternoon by the time the convoy crossed the border. We were still a good way from Lusaka, where we would be joined by our Zambian counterparts, refuel and change our

32

rands for kwachas. The supply truck was ordered to drive along the Chipata road for 150 kilometres, find a camp site and start preparing the evening meal.

No sooner said than done. It was dark by the time we passed the last squatter shacks on the outskirts of Lusaka. We sped on into the night. Ferdi showed his prowess behind the wheel and I remained on the lookout for stretches of tar between the potholes. Those potholes could swallow an entire truck. If you saw any cat's-eye road reflectors around here, you could be reasonably sure it was a giraffe standing in a pothole! On dark African roads you usually have to keep a constant watch for bewildered, blinded animals, but tonight nothing appeared in our headlights.

When we had covered more or less 150 kilometres, we found ourselves in a dense mopane forest on a road with high shoulders. We stopped and I walked ahead in search of a suitable spot to turn off the road. About two hundred metres into the bush we found a camping spot that would accommodate the convoy.

With the vehicle switched off, an unnatural silence fell over the bush. It was as if the place was devoid of night sounds. The weather was warm and sultry. We soon realised that the convoy would not be able to see us from the road and, chatting cheerfully, we walked to the roadside with two rolls of toilet paper. There we created a white paper Christmas scene. Nobody would pass this way without seeing us.

We unloaded the tables, built huge fires and prepared the meal. By the time we had finished, it was close to midnight and there was still no sign of the convoy. Ferdi went to sleep and I waited, while squadrons of mosquitoes converged on our camp site. The absolute silence amazed me – had the people around here eaten all the animals?

It was after one in the morning when a vehicle burst through our toilet paper banners and trimmings. I charged to the road – in the Land Cruiser was Dr Kumzuma of Zambia Nature Conservation, bearing the news that the convoy had been delayed in

Lusaka and would be spending the night there. What was more, we were to return immediately – our camp site was three kilometres from the Mozambican border and Renamo troops had killed four people there the day before.

Ferdi and I conferred. The table had been laid, food had been prepared for more than sixty people, everything had been unpacked and it was impossible to cover the 150 kilometres back to Lusaka on bad roads before first light. No, we would take our chances and stay here. The doctor took his leave and an almost palpable silence settled over us again.

What now? Ferdi had been driving all day and needed to sleep. I sent him to bed. I would stand guard. My only weapons were an axe and a spade. I removed the paper decorations and extinguished the fires – all the while knowing that it was too late! There was no way the soldiers had not been aware of us all along. My own wartime experience had taught me that you move away from a "soft target", look in from the outside and let things develop. The truck – with Ferdi and me, the cheery tables and the pots of food – was one of the softest targets imaginable, and I hoped the convoy would still find us here tomorrow morning.

It was still hot and muggy. I took off my shirt, grabbed my weapons, moved about fifteen metres away and lay down with my bum in a thornbush. If Renamo stormed the camp, my plan was to surprise them from behind, knocking them down with the spade.

The mosquitoes seemed determined to carry me off. Searching for repellent in the dark, I found only a bottle of rum. Dejectedly I emptied the bottle over my back, chest and arms and took up my position again.

Later I heard from Ferdi that he had looked out in the early hours to see if his protector was still holding the fort. In the light of his torch he saw me lying with my head resting on the spade, fast asleep. A cloud of mosquitoes billowed around me, but the strange thing was . . . They settled on my naked torso, gave a few licks and then flew away in a drunken stupor.

And I told him . . .

And I told him: "Fuck off!" He stood around sheepishly, saliva drooling from the corner of his mouth.

"Fuck off, shoo, go away, bugger off!" And from his threadbare pocket he produced two dry heads of maize and placed them on a used paper plate next to the fire and shuffled misshapenly into the bush . . .

Kalie is a farmer, and a successful one too. That was why he and I were able to bum around in Barotseland, Western Zambia, in an expensive air-conditioned 4x4. We did this often, the two of us.

Barotseland is probably one of the poorest parts of Africa that I have ever visited. It's understandable, actually, for the Litunga, the king of the Balozi, who inhabit these parts, refuses to accept the authority of Lusaka. Kaunda and his successor, Chiluba, have therefore deliberately disinvested in the region. But it is rich in natural beauty, with the mighty Zambezi River rising here, and winding its leisurely way across flood plains to the sea.

Barotseland is to hell and gone, and a lack of infrastructure and the war in Angola have caused efforts at tourism and development to fail. Empty lodges and holiday resorts are the order of the day. One is struck, however, by the friendliness of the people and, despite the poverty, the absence of typically African beggars, with hands reaching out hopelessly at passing wealth.

Our vehicle was loaded with fine food and cold drinks. We drove through the destitution in style.

All efforts at farming seemed doomed here. The mahango and maize fields stood cropless and shrivelled.

Kalie remarked: "Modern technological development and Africa will probably never find each other. Not even a mighty river with more water than all the South African rivers put together is capable of making its people win the battle against drought."

Actually I was fed up with Kalie. He had brought along bags of sweets and Boxer tobacco to distribute to poverty-stricken Africa. Personally I don't believe you can save Africa with sweets. You only spoil the people and teach them to beg. Livingstone and his band of missionaries buggered up Africa's equilibrium like that. I had taken charge of the sweets, and the tobacco was coming in handy because my own supply of smokes was depleted.

I must admit, however, that the poverty was shocking. Every ragged child held a piece of dried maize in his hand, with which he attempted to appease his hunger kernel by kernel. It was the daily ration, we learned.

We travelled deeper into the bush. After we had crossed the Zambezi by ferry, we emerged on the flood plains. These plains are beautiful – devoid of trees and with waving grass as far as the eye can see. The water was rising and the Balozi traditionally move to higher ground around this time.

We pitched camp under a stand of trees. We settled in. Arranged tables and chairs. The fire was stacked high. Drinks were poured and, while the African night engulfed us, we spoke about adventure, about enjoyment and being privileged, about poverty and begging. That was when I shat on Kalie about the sweets.

Snug under my mosquito net, I gazed at the stars and dozed off.

I got up early and started the coffee. Then he came walking through the bush. Perhaps "walking" is not the right word – "shambling" is a more accurate description.

Scarecrow-tattered, face distorted in a spasm, hand lamely deformed. Laughing inanely, he stood there, mumbling incoherently. Not a welcome sight for any traveller on an empty stomach.

I'll get rid of him quickly, I thought, and shoved a bag of sweets into his hand. "Thank you, goodbye, sela gabotse, auf Wiedersehn," I waved him on his way.

Foolish and retarded, he raised his semifunctioning hand and shuffled off into the bush, mouth gaping.

As I was lighting my pipe with relish, steaming coffee in hand, he was back again. And I told him: "Fuck off!" And he placed a two-day supply of his own food in front of me and fucked off.

The kukri

His mother and father and I just about grew up together. I say "just about", because actually our respective fathers were hunting partners. Not hunting in a modern context, in their case. They did it the way it was done two centuries ago. Buffalo and elephant, lion and leopard. Hunting expeditions that lasted for three months, somewhere in German East Africa or Portuguese West Africa.

During those times we came from the Colony to stay with them in the Transvaal. My mom sent us to nursery school with them and we, West Coast children, learned about city kids. They ate grated carrots for lunch and were forced to take an afternoon nap – there was no playing on the beach in the afternoons and bringing home mussels.

The British, in their thirst for world domination, made use of vanquished or colonised nations to serve as canon fodder in their imperialist army. There were the Irish, who "took the penny", the Indians, who tried to chase the Germans out of Tanzania at Tanga, the Australians, who fell in droves at Gallipoli, the South African Red Tabs, who surrendered at Tobruk, and then there were the Gurkhas. Fearless Nepalese. They were the assassin forces of the British. They were the ones who moved in behind the lines and soundlessly slit the throats of the enemy.

Every man chooses his own path, but paths are known to cross, and we three children of bygone days met up with one another again. The two of them were married with children and I had my own crew. Now that we were older, a firm friendship developed. Our visits usually ended with tales about hunting, guns, knives and other subjects close to an Afrikaner boy's heart. I was aware of the little boy, listening enthralled to stories about his grandfathers and his father and lovingly stroking a rifle or a beautiful knife.

To kill a man noiselessly you need a good knife. The Gurkhas' traditional weapon is the kukri, a long knife with a slightly curved blade, razor-sharp, with a notch at the base of the blade. It is heavy and can serve as a bush knife, to clear a path through the jungle.

The little boy was barely fourteen when the doctors announced that his father was dying; time left together was limited. In front of my eyes a big, active man of the veld changed into a shrunken, emaciated invalid. This brush with death influenced us all. The men withdrew. My wife, a psychologist, stepped in, took his hand and accompanied him on his journey to meet death. We hunters, who had often been killers ourselves, no longer had any desire to spend time together and invented furtive excuses not to talk about rifles and knives any more.

And somewhere along the line the little boy disappeared as well.

To escape, I went to Nepal. Rambling around in the kingdom of the mountains made me forget about death at home. In Katmandu I came across a kukri. To recognise a good kukri, you have to know something about knives. The heavy Gurkha knife has a certain point of balance and you test it by balancing it on your finger. I bought a beautiful specimen, razor-sharp and well balanced. At home I hung it on the wall – it was too beautiful to lock away in a safe.

At his father's funeral the boy was sullen and apparently unemotional. He kept his distance, as if he knew that the role of carer would now be resting on his fifteen-year-old shoulders. His mother had to do her bit to keep the wolf from the door and he said farewell to puberty alone and defiantly. Now and then he would call on my wife. What they discussed, I had no idea.

He was in matric when I came home one day to find that the kukri was missing. When I learned that he had come round earlier, I knew at once what had happened to it. My first reaction was to fly into a blind rage. But I realised that this was a private matter between him and me.

The next day during school hours, I had him summoned on the intercom while I waited outside. A tall young man came sauntering towards me, his hands pushed into his pockets. He was clearly ill at ease. I could see his father in him. When he saw me, his bravado and nonchalance started to wane.

"My boy, don't even try to feed me shit today," I plunged straight in. "I know it's just about the most beautiful knife a man could ever hold in his hand. Where is it, so that I can fetch it?"

He opened his mouth half-heartedly to protest. "If you're honest with me, no one will ever know about it," I added.

The almost-man became a little boy as he told me where it was.

As I turned to leave, he spoke in a soft voice: "Oom, I miss my dad."

My brother's keeper

"Kalie is gone," she told me. "It's *your* fault – go look for him."

What keeps me sane, is occasionaly escaping from what is considered normal. As a safari operator, I happen to show people the wild places of our continent. Ordinary people. People who pound away at a typewriter – these days a word processor – every day. Or who beat a path to the deeds office. Or who have to placate disgruntled customers.

In my company they have learned what it means to get away from it all.

Kalie farms. He started out on a combine harvester in a High-veld mealie field; later he began to cultivate grapes somewhere outside Stellenbosch for Dad. To farm on behalf of Dad, brothers and the rest, is no easy feat. "You'd better not stuff up our inheritance!" he was told.

Breaking free from the constraints of normality takes guts. Sometimes it starts with a small step. Just saying "I want to" can be hard. It's even harder to return to reality and normality.

In gumboots vines were planted in the clayey soil. The family farm became a jewel; brothers were having a ball and Dad was growing older and more full of shit. And Kalie kept farming, without respite.

Shaking off your responsibilities, even temporarily, makes you think of what you have and don't have. Joining in my adventures has seen many marital bonds suffer a setback. Many have ended up losing their jobs and for some abusing the bottle was the start of a downward spiral – for them returning to normality was no longer an option. Still, lonely people have formed lifelong friendships, single people have found partners and some returned to their mundane existence with newfound gusto.

It was after twelve years of thankless labour that Kalie phoned one day: "Ouboet, that longstanding invitation sounds about right to me now – I'm coming along."

And together we hiked through the Fish River canyon. And later the Naukluft. And later Kilimanjaro. And later the Himala-

43

yas. And later we drove through Kaokoland. And later he drove through the Richtersveld on his own. And Botswana. And the high mountains of Lesotho.

And when Miranda said "Go look for him", I did as I was told.

And never returned myself.

Angel

She came walking towards me through the sand in the moonlight. I thought I recognised her. She was wearing a long, flowing dress, and a straw hat pulled deep over her eyes . . .

It was a quarter to three in the morning and I was lying in my sleeping bag somewhere beside the lower Fish River in Namibia. I did not feel well – in actual fact, I felt extremely unwell. I knew from experience what was wrong – I was dehydrated. The desert sun and the gruelling days of hiking unremittingly over skull-shaped rocks, sand and boulders had taken their toll. My worn-out body, which I had systematically been reducing to ruin over the years, was protesting.

Once again we were in the middle of an inexplicable adventure. Once again we had tackled the near-impossible. The idea had been to start at Seeheim and walk along the banks of the Fish River, through the canyon, to where it joined up with the Orange River – a distance of 300 kilometres. Even worse – all this had to be done in only ten days, in other words at a rate of 30 kilometres per day. Crazy . . .

It was day nine, we had another 40 kilometres to go, and it looked as if the hike was over for me. I was losing fluid in every possible way. From the top, the bottom and even the middle. We had already lost Daan, and my comrades Kalie and Mario were anxiously trying to fill me up with fluids, for in that desert region they would either have to carry me out or cover me with rocks – no humans ever came there.

I watched her approach through narrowed eyes. Was it time to be fetched? I thought I recognised her . . .

My mind wandered . . .

I saw her for the first time when she grabbed my hand somewhere on a cliff in the Witels. I was on my own, jumping, climbing and swimming to Ceres, doing what is known as "kloofing". I had left the group behind. We were behind schedule, as we had been snowed in in the Hex River mountains. An urgent appointment had made me act irresponsibly. On a rocky ledge fourteen metres above the river a stone had become dislodged, my backpack had pulled me over the edge, but suddenly there was a handhold.

I think she had brown eyes when she laughed.

My bakkie had broken down somewhere between the Ugab and the Brandberg. My technical know-how is limited to fuel supply and spark. I'm buggered, I thought, I won't get out alive. No one knew that I was there alone. Dejectedly I sat down on a rock, while she fiddled under the hood. With a laugh she shook her brown hair back, a greasy smudge on her nose.

The mission hospital at Ngoma in Malawi had crawled with the sick and deformed. Malaria was consuming me piece by piece. I was pissing blood. Black water fever? it flashed through my mind. The bouts of fever came and went with monotonous regularity, and I felt that I was slowly becoming detached from reality.

"Have you come to fetch me?" I asked her as she sat down at the foot of my bed.

"Not yet," she answered with a sad smile, one eyelid drooping slightly.

This hike had been one of the toughest of my life. The terrain was merciless and the heat blistering – it descended from above just to be hurled back from the ground. We tried to get most of the walking behind us in the early morning, when the air was cooler. At noon we searched for any bit of shade that rock or boulder afforded, and continued later in a gentler sun.

This river and its canyon remained one of the most remarkable places on our planet, and we found pleasure in knowing no one had ever tackled the route in this way before. The age-old rock walls and formations towered vertically around us. A small herd of Hartmann zebra looked inquisitively at the strange creatures hurrying through their world. We were ecstatic to discover that Namibia had another finger rock that no one knew about!

The evenings were the highlight, however, when we threw down our rucksacks, lit a fire and poured a stiff drink. With the pleasure of camaraderie, we joked about the day's hardships.

But now I didn't know – another hot day like today was going to break me. So near yet so far. Had I overplayed my hand at last?

She knelt beside me.

"It's all right. Things will work out," she consoled me. She took me in her arms, kissed me on the forehead and cried.

And when the day broke, it was overcast and raining in the desert. And I walked to the bridge at the Orange River – "One-two-three, block myself" – and wondered if it had been her last visit . . .

Calculate the cost

One moment we were struggling down the dry river bed and forcing the vehicles back up the bank. The next moment we were racing across a gravel plain to avoid a bend in the river. When we approached the river bed for a second attempt at crossing – a seething mass of water lay in front of us . . .

Men like Hillary, Amundsen, Speke and Burton had captured my imagination from an early age. Westerners who had been brave enough to discover unknown parts of our planet. But Hillary had stood on top of Everest three years before I even saw the light – in other words, by the time I had grown up, there was absolutely bugger all left for me to discover.

It had become an obsession to go in search of places where my neighbours and their families had never been and would never want to be. I had often succeeded, but here in South Africa there had been an annoying turn of events. I call it "the Getaway syndrome". All my old playing fields were being tamed by the publication of articles that attracted a swarm of "adventurers". It had developed into a race: I tried to get to an exceptional place before them, and briefly made it mine.

"Boeta, I'm inviting Kalie and you for a visit," the invitation came.

And a dream I'd had for years took shape. A dream to stand way up north, at Angra Fria on the Skeleton Coast. Up to now it had been no more than a dream, for ordinary people are not allowed to enter there.

Luck plays a considerable role if you go in search of the lesser known, for the man who had invited us was my own brother Chrisjan, who was managing a concession area in the Skeleton Coast Park in Namibia for Wilderness Safaris.

It was early morning when we pushed the nose of the Land Cruiser northward and crossed the Piekeniers Pass to Noordoewer. A hell of a distance lay ahead, but our plan was to find our way to the rendezvous with Chrisjan in Oom Japie's pub at Kamanjab unhurriedly, travelling along the back roads.

The first starry night found us lying in bed rolls beside a blazing fire at the mouth of the Gamkab canyon, on the banks of the Orange. Before the "G-factor", few people had known about this isolated spot. We cracked a bottle of Bonnies and drank to what lay ahead . . .

Between Aus and Helmeringhausen our GPS pointed out "an alternative route" and we knew the G-factor had not discovered it yet, so we took it . . . It was the most beautiful time of day. Bat-eared foxes romped and raced across the red dunes, the bushman grass was tinged by the late afternoon sun. We were alone – there were no other tracks in the road. Friend Kalie and I drank a toast and grinned broadly.

At Swakop we enjoyed a beer and Hackbrötchen. We played pool in the De Duine Hotel at Henties. At Spitzkoppe we outwitted the G-factor by pitching our tent at Kleine Spitzkopf and in solitude we watched the earth swallow the sun.

The reunion with Kleinboet was a happy one. We don't see each other often. He had been in the Kaokoland desert for six years. He knew those parts like the back of his hand. He enjoyed a position of trust among the Himbas and he knew the desert elephants by name.

Cousin Danne was also with Chrisjan and in two vehicles we sped off to Grootberg. Somewhere on top of the pass we drove into the bushes, lit a huge fire and, fortified by a shot of whisky, Chrisjan told us about the last no-man's-land in this southern land. Nature Conservation had declared the region an off-limits nature reserve. He told us about a group of tourists who had ignored all warnings and gone into the reserve. He and the men from Nature Conservation had followed their tracks, which would be a silent reminder of their destructive behaviour for many years, caught them and handed them over to the police. All their vehicles and equipment had been confiscated, they had each been fined R10 000 and deported as personae non gratae. Clearly you didn't go looking for trouble around there – not even if you were a G-factor enthusiast.

In the early hours the heavens opened suddenly and it rained.

We threw our bedding into the vehicles and scrummed down around the valiant fire while the water poured over us in bucketfuls. We sang and danced like demented baboons, knowing it was the desert and tomorrow everything would be dry again.

That was true as we drove through the dry Hoanib just past the Khowarib Schlucht. Chrisjan was uneasy. He knew if it had rained higher up, the rivers of Kaokoland would come down in flood and we could be stranded for days.

The moment of truth arrived when we reached the Skelm River. This little stream rises high up in the mountains east of Warmquelle and flows into the Hoanib near Sesfontein. The locals were standing around, unable to cross.

We didn't have much time. We two brothers waded through. The water came up to our balls, but the current was strong and tugged at our legs. Boeta was in a hurry to show us his world. He pushed the nose of his bakkie into the river, but failed to reach the opposite bank. The river began to play with the bakkie. Water poured in through the windows. We charged in and I could feel the sand being swept from under the wheels.

We're going to lose the vehicle, it crossed my mind, and I called out to Kalie to bring the larger Cruiser so that we could pull the bakkie out.

On the opposite bank at last, we poured a stiff gin to put a stop to the worst shivering. I pushed a CD into the player and Valiant Swart sang:

"As jy anderkant haal, dan moet jy wys en betaal, en as jy terug wil kom . . . gaan maak maar self daai som" – If you reach the other side, you'll have to confess and pay the price and if you want to return . . . you'll have to calculate the cost.

And I wondered how prophetic those words would be.

Now we were standing at Purros and in front of us the Hoarusib was in flood, a seething brown mass that swept along everything in its path. Where we were standing, it was as wide as the Orange. It was an awesome sight. We looked at one another . . .

That night the mosquitoes were a nuisance and I didn't sleep much – had we reached the turning point?

Was the Skeleton Coast eluding me? I wondered as I tossed and turned. Beside me Chrisjan was also struggling to settle down . . .

But if a man really puts his mind to something, he can do it, and around noon we decided that we were going to give it a try. The river had run down considerably, but we were afraid of the next deluge and we tied the vehicles together with towropes. Adrenaline pumped as we ploughed through mud, weeds and water and reached the opposite bank with roaring engines.

And if you want to return, you'll have to calculate the cost . . .

And we drove into the desert and it was so beautiful and so solitary and we were so privileged and I understood why my brother was unable to return – where could a nature lover like him find anything better?

We drove through a sea of shifting dunes, we climbed up basalt hills and looked far into our futures, we walked across salt pans to meet our past, we found the shelters of the Strandlopers that are hundreds of years old, we frolicked with seals in the icy waters of Cape Fria and washed up with the wrecks at the mouth of the Khumib, we picked up handfuls of agate and amethyst and let them run through our fingers, we sat around fires till late, encompassed by the starry skies, we laughed and we cried and we discovered, like the travellers of old . . . And I knew we had already calculated the cost: we had rediscovered friendship, brotherhood and camaraderie.

A different kind of Christmas

I was still opening my present (I happened to know it was a Bible), when kleinboet Christian toddled through the glass door on the stoep. In front of my eyes the window shattered and a shard fell from above like a guillotine, piercing his upper lip. He was only two years old and couldn't understand all the blood and the screaming. It was the first Christmas Eve I can really remember. That evening in my eleventh year I dedicated my life to the Lord – please let Boetie live – as I carefully took the glass spear out of his palate and picked him up and handed him to Ma and Pa like an offering.

My mother, Margaret, believed that Christmas Eve was a Bakkes evening – as a family we would open our presents; we would be together. All her chicks under her wing. But she hadn't taken into account what she had created, for it certainly wasn't potatoes that she had planted and raised. Each of us, Marius, Christian, Matilde and I, had a yearning to seek out new horizons and to do things our own way . . .

On Christmas Eve 1982 I found myself in Oshakati, Sector One Zero, Vamboland. A few comrades and I had just liberated three chickens from a nearby village. The logistics men at the bulk supply shed had liberated a bottle or two of booze. Tonight we were going to celebrate Christmas – the troops in the observation towers of Alpha Company were on the lookout and would stop the enemy in their tracks . . .

On the fire the chickens became burnt offerings to Thor as we mounted the Buffels. For the soldiers at Oshivello, Christmas Eve had got off to a blazing start – 61 Mechanical Brigade was under fire and looking for support. It was no "Silent Night" for Swapo. I remember the wild look in my comrades' eyes – what a Christmas gift it would be to survive . . .

We hung scraps of white paper from the thorns of the acacia that extended its branches like a crucifix over the Kwando flood plains. It would be our Christmas tree tonight. The quiet of the Western Caprivi settled in our hearts.

The elephant herd was unaware of our camp site. They were

lumbering towards the river and heading straight for us. It was a large herd – about two hundred strong, the matriarch sniffing, her trunk raised like an antenna. I remember Pottie saying softly: "Don't fuck with the king." And then the wind turned and they were upon us and they were charging and trumpetting and we were shouting and beating on pots and lids and we knew if we ran now, it would be the end; and we stood our ground and they veered past. That evening my Christmas gift was a handshake, wrapped in friendship.

A white Christmas. It was bitterly cold – all year round in these parts. We were somewhere on the slopes of Numbur, a sacred mountain for the Sherpas of the Himalayas. We were lying in – actually we were snowed in. There was no escape. Certainly not tonight. Kalie and I lay snuggled up in the two-man tent that was buckling under the weight of the snow. When one hip gave in, we said "turn", and we turned and faced the other side. "Boeta, do you realise it's Christmas Eve?" I asked, and he pulled off his gloves and with chapped, frozen fingers and chattering teeth, he cooked barley on the primus – the most delicious Christmas dinner I had ever enjoyed.

"It's going to be a dry Christmas," I realised, as the captain in the Mauritanian army stopped our bus and pulled us over. I meant it literally as well as figuratively, for in the Islamic Republic of Mauritania alcohol is forbidden. We got out and the sifting Sahara sand filtered through our desert headdresses.

"Your cholera injection has lapsed," said the man, as he looked through my papers. I knew he wanted a bribe, for inoculation against cholera was no longer mandatory. Surreptitiously I pressed a few wads into his hand. Not every person can buy his freedom on Christmas Eve . . .

And then? As life went on, and what used to be adventurous and different became tedious, and loved ones who had been away returned . . . you got the team together. "Tonight it's going to be only us on Christmas Eve, the way my mother taught me."

And Nanna roasted a leg of lamb and my son, Marc, built

the fire and Cara, my daughter, sang. And one more time Mary explained to Joseph why they had to sleep in the stable tonight and men arrived with scented stuff and knick-knacks and even the farmhands left their sheep somewhere in the Ceres Bo-Karoo and Herod was out to kill. And you sat back contentedly and thought: What a different kind of Christmas!

And then Marc walked through the glass door.

The apricot lady of Nouadhibou

Nouadhibou is like an octopus, with tentacles that pull you in time and again.

Ferdi and I once again found ourselves in the dusty streets of this godforsaken place, swaddled in cloths to keep out the Saharan sand and grit that penetrated everywhere. We looked at each other dejectedly. Where to now? A beer would be nice, but where would we find one in this hellhole on the northern border of the Islamic Republic of Mauritania?

A sand-bitten signboard caught our eye: *Hotel Magareb.*

We looked at each other again and wordlessly began to push against the Harmattan wind . . .

We opened the door of the hotel, and a cool, dark reception area welcomed us. In the dim light I saw a black man behind the counter. Slavery had been officially abolished in these parts only fifteen years earlier, but black people still remained slaves.

Our French was limited to "Bonjour, monsieur . . . bière?"

The man looked up, surprised, and smiled. He motioned to the left and led the way. At a small bar with a few tables he stepped behind the counter, though the liquor cabinet did not contain any bottles.

The barman introduced himself as Yaccob from the Ivory Coast and miraculously produced two cold Dutch beers. We ripped off our Touareg headdresses and gulped down the beer hastily without asking the price. A second round appeared on the counter and Yaccob pushed a cassette into a dilapidated tape recorder – the most beautiful music from his part of the world. On the corner of the counter lay a tattered magazine with Ché Guevara on the cover. It was French, and when I paged through it, I saw an article with illustrations of different sexual positions from the Kamasutra.

We have been "in country" for a long time, I thought . . . We had been trying to cross the border to Morocco for ten days – a dream of travelling through Africa from south to north using public road transport had landed us here. The Polisario Front wanted Western Sahara, but Morocco would not give in.

The desert was full of landmines and the Mauritanians had closed their border posts, we heard on our arrival. After a thirteen-hour journey from hell through Southern Sahara in a packed Mauritanian four-by-four this news was not received well. But a Boer makes a plan, even if he finds himself to hell 'n gone at the back of beyond.

Enquiries about alternative methods of crossing the border put us in contact with the Nouadhibou underworld. "Yes, at a price we'll smuggle you across the Mauritanian border and past the military posts and take you through the landmines to the Moroccan gun emplacements and army posts."

Money changed hands. For days we heard nothing from our would-be guides. Then one night they arrived at the place where we were staying and took us to a windowless hovel somewhere deep in a residential area with houses built of mud. We were certain it was the last we would ever see of our money. For forty-eight hours we lay in the dark, sombre house, waiting for further news. We could not go out, for the moment we stuck our heads through the door a horde of Islamic kids pelted the white infidels with stones.

Late one night we were picked up in an open "garrie". Our guide and driver was Mohammed and with him was a lieutenant of the Polisario Front's military wing, disguised as an ordinary Mauritanian. We sat in the back. The desert wind was cold when at last we shook off the dust of Nouadhibou. At border and police posts whispered negotiations took place and we were allowed through. The dream was coming to life! Now only the military posts and the landmines remained. Somewhere in the deep Sahara we covered ourselves with our desert cloths and slept, sand heaping up against us.

When the sun came out, the Land Rover was making a dash for the border at high speed. We were hoping the Mauritanian soldiers would still be asleep. When at last we stopped behind a high dune and Mohammed surveyed our surroundings, I realised we were in no-man's-land and landmine territory. It was obvious from the exploded wreckage lying all around us. Then we saw them on a dune in the distance: the Moroccan gun emplacements. The vehicle got stuck, and we had to push and throw out sand ladders. Our own war had taught us that in landmine country you stick to old tracks. Where we had to push, we were careful not to step outside the tracks of the vehicle.

At last the military boom. We had made it.

Just to be told: "Gentlemen, except for Mauritanians, no African passport holders are allowed to pass through – this is a war zone."

Ferdi and I moved to a table with more beer, the magazine forgotten on the counter. Yaccob disappeared and we sat enjoying the music.

Suddenly she appeared in the doorway. With finely chiselled features and neatly dressed in an apricot-coloured outfit. Gracefully she walked to the counter. I saw a glimpse of a white undergarment beneath the silky blouse and I caught a whiff of apricot blossoms. She greeted sedately and sat down. While having a quiet conversation with Yaccob, who had put in an appearance again, she paged distractedly through the magazine. I immediately caught on to the game – the coincidence of Yaccob having left the room only to reappear immediately after her entrance . . . the provocative contents of the magazine . . .

Nature called and I excused myself. On my return, the lady was deep in conversation with my friend Ferdi – the choice had been made. I joined them. She spoke English and I detected breeding and education. She was from Ghana and life had washed her ashore here with her ten-year-old daughter. Her greatest wish was to escape from this barren, godforsaken desert region. Mine too, I thought to myself. In her eyes I recognised longing for the jungles of her home country.

With an entreating gesture she turned to Ferdi. Suddenly he understood and began to speak about a wife and children in the distant south. As he rambled on, the woman in front of me

61

became visibly weary. Her shoulders slumped. The hand she had extended to him went slack as he hammered in one nail after another. In an attempt to soften the blow, I gently promised to look after her if ever she arrived on my doorstep in South Africa.

We got up and paid. She stopped me at the door and thrust a piece of paper into my hand. The blinding desert sun nearly knocked us off our feet and I could scarcely make out the words: *I am Helen and thank you.*

Two days later we were sprinting across the runway to a waiting plane. If this place never saw me again, it would be too soon.

On the steps I looked round one last time. On the other side of the fence the apricot lady of Nouadhibou stood waving.

Beautiful

I noticed her while I was in the process of taking a photo. From somewhere outside the lens. And I was instantly ice-cold and dismayed by the accusation in her eye. Hurriedly I took the photo and disappeared into the crowd.

Guiltily I hastened through the throng in the market place of Londuimbali. The place was teeming. I pushed into an alley, shouldered an old man out of my way and nearly stumbled over a small child. When I looked up, I saw her again, looking at me from a distance . . . I pushed to the left, into the next alley, taking no notice of the brightly stacked, fresh vegetables and fruit, or the newly baked loaves, steaming in a dish. I was moving more slowly now, with lowered head. When I looked up again, there she was, gazing at me . . .

A market in Africa draws me like a magnet. The maze of streets and stalls enthralls me. I can soak up the colours, smells and bustle of sellers, wares and buyers for hours. Superficially all markets look the same, but if you scratch more deeply, each tells the story of its country, its village, its people, its suffering, its good, its evil and its pleasures.

Markets? I'll never forget the brassiere stalls of Kalomo in Zambia. White, red, purple, pink and blue ones, new ones, old ones and four-times-used ones. My German clients were afraid. They found the crowds, the filth and the squalor repulsive.

At the market in Karogo in the north of the Ivory Coast, I stared open-mouthed at the livestock enclosure. Flanked by weavers and coppersmiths, you could buy a sheep or goat, dead or alive, depending on how you wanted it packaged. I recall with horror how I witnessed a suspected pickpocket being stoned to death by traders. It was anything but a pretty sight.

In the labyrinth that is the medina at Fes, past the souks selling beautiful leather and copper wares, carpets and perfume, I also found the hashish dens and saw the underbelly of Morocco, surrounded by rats and human excrement . . .

This second trip through Angola was a retracing of history

for me. Unlike my previous visit eight months before, when I had gone back on the trail of the Dorsland trekkers, I was retracing my own footsteps this time. I had returned to *feel* the desctruction of this former African jewel. My comrades and I had been part of it, had *helped* to destroy it. We had known places like Ongiva, Xangongo, Cuvelai and Calai; we had helped shoot them to pieces. It hadn't stopped there, unfortunately, for when we had left, the Angolans had carried on destroying one another.

As our journey progressed, I became more and more depressed. Roads were in poor shape, buildings were crumbling, people were defeated. Young men were conspicuous in their absence, I noticed. But what could one expect after a war that had lasted for 25 years?

I disregarded the beautiful scenery and focused instead on the blown-up vehicles and bullet-riddled tanks at the roadside. The incredible coastline, palm tree oases and deltas passed by unnoticed. I was on the lookout for landmines. Corrupt bureaucrats and policemen caused me to ignore the friendly, smiling population. Large-scale economic collapse and decline made me blind to the efforts of those who were trying to piece their lives together again.

Now I was looking for something beautiful to photograph, a colourful image of a beautiful woman in traditional dress, I thought, as I stopped at the market place of Londuimbali. I grabbed my camera.

It was market day and everyone was there. I was enthralled by the atmosphere. I strolled around – not unnoticed, because very few visitors ever stop there. I studied the women surreptitiously. Each carried a child on the hip, even young girls of about fourteen. A new nation was being built.

A beautiful girl caught my eye. Exquisite in patterned yellow, with a bright orange headscarf. She had beautiful eyes.

"May I take your picture?" I asked and knew she didn't understand. I pointed at the camera.

"Fotografia?" I tried in Portuguese. She smiled coyly and I took the photograph.

"Obrigada."

Another beautiful woman captured my lens. Shyly she peered around a corner.

Another one, and suddenly I had an entire entourage.

They're getting more and more beautiful, I thought, and selected only the prettiest.

I stopped a tall, elegant woman – she radiated a defiant nobility. High cheekbones, long, dangling earrings, smouldering. It was as I was about to take the photograph . . . from the corner of my eye I saw her standing at a distance. The stark disfigurement shocked me. Half her face was missing. There was only one eye, and she was looking at me, and the eye was saying: "What about me? I know you don't find me beautiful, so you won't take my picture."

I left.

It became a nightmare, for wherever I turned, she loomed in front of me. I hurried back to the car – I couldn't bear any more ugliness. I unlocked the door. There was a hand on my shoulder. I swung round and looked into the hollow eye of ruin.

Then she turned her unscathed side towards me and the person standing in front of me smiled and handed me a bunch of frangipani.

I did not take her photograph. That kind of beauty cannot be captured on film.

Justice always prevails

"Bruce, don't you think it's time for bed?" The words came softly, guardedly, from one of the tents.

We had built a huge fire. Piet and I gave each other knowing glances. There were two reasons why Bruce, seated at the fire with us, could not go to bed at that moment. Firstly, he was so smashed that he could not get up. Secondly, a pack of hyenas were snuffling around in the space between the fire and the tents . . .

I had known Bruce longer than I knew Piet, my safari partner. In fact, Bruce and I had studied together – the hard way. He was an attorney's clerk, and I worked for a firm of auditors. In the evenings we studied extramurally at Tukkies, trying to get our papers. There was really no time for play – it was working and swotting, working and swotting. "But one day . . ." the two of us had vowed. When we did manage to break away a little, it was difficult. He was married and I was trying to court my girl. Eventually his marriage bit the dust, while I was still trying to court my girl.

Piet and I, armed with spades and burning embers, were trying to keep the hyenas away from the tents. We realised it was going to be a struggle to get Bruce to his tent. All the clients were in bed; he was the only one who had stubbornly refused to retire to the apparent safety of the tent he shared with Ina.

Ina, pretty as a picture and stylish, who had rescued him from the chaos of our survivor's existence of those days. Established in her profession, she gently put him back on track. Perhaps Bruce had been reluctant to expose Ina to our unnatural lifestyle, because I never really got to know her. Until the day that I had said: "I'm taking a group of clients to Botswana. Do you want to come along?"

We had finished our studies. Professionally qualified, each had gone his own way. My career had unravelled. The bush had always attracted me. Induku Safaris was an excuse for Piet and me to venture into the wild. We preferred doing it the hard way. Open trucks, tents, clients who cooked for themselves and helped pitch camp. If we got stuck, or had a flat tyre, everyone pitched in. "Africa is not for sissies," was our motto. That was why I was somewhat surprised to see Ina at our departure, clad in a loose-fitting white trouser suit, high heels, straw hat and scarf, and dragging along a trolley case.

"Bliksem, Bruce," I pulled him aside. "Did you at least pack some goggles for her? I told you you'd be spending most of the trip on the back of an open Bedford, didn't I?"

He produced some welding goggles that looked like a glass diving mask, with a dark section that could be tipped up.

"This is mine. I told her we would be travelling with air conditioning and sleeping in luxury lodges – otherwise she'd never have agreed to come."

I just shook my head. There were thirty people in our group, and in the end she was his responsibility, I hoped.

One truck broke down just before we reached Vaalwater and it was late at night when the exhausted convoy came to a halt at the closed Groblersbrug border post. Tents were pitched on the grass between the policemen's lavatories.

Ina didn't say a word.

The next morning she emerged from their two-man tent, dressed in sparkling white. Beautifully turned out. A Vogue cover girl, I thought. Bruce himself was wearing white overalls, the welding mask perched on his head as if he was some kind of First World War pilot. Liquor was not included in our rates, and at Sherwood Ranch, just across the border, Bruce bought six crates of beer.

Ina didn't say a word.

At Nata water pressure was a problem and washing facilities were limited, but in the morning Ina came out to greet the new day, immaculately dressed in yet another new outfit. The welding mask now had a permanent place on top of Bruce's head. Clad in his overalls, he started taking his liquid refreshments early in the day.

Ina didn't say a word.

On the back of the Bedford the white overalls turned brown, while Ina gazed into the bushes, her hand clutching her straw hat. As Bruce grew dirtier and drunker, Ina seemed to become prettier and more chic. Bruce drank with a vengeance – it was as if he wanted to drown all the suffering of the past. And the welding mask was permanently on his forehead, the dark section tipped up like the antenna of an insect.

And Ina didn't say a word.

The Savuti is known for its elephants that come marauding through the camps in search of oranges and water that careless tourists have fed them in the past. A bigger problem, however, was the nightly visits of hyenas. During previous trips they had carried off the clients' leather bags and bitten holes in cool boxes. That was why, when everyone had anxiously retired to bed, Piet and I were on guard – and of course there was Bruce.

"Bruce, don't you think it's time for bed?" Ina's voice came from the tent. As if for the first time she wanted to say that enough was enough. I heard the fear and uncertainty in her voice and chased off the scavengers, while Piet helped Bruce to his feet. Like a sack of potatoes we bundled him into the tent.

It became a long night for Piet and me. Wood on the fire, driving away the hyenas, dozing off, coffee. Finally first light. In the dawn hours we took a nap beside the fire. Then a blood-curdling scream . . .

"Ag, jirre, help! I'm blind!"

A deathly silence fell. Piet and I struggled to our feet, half dazed. Outside the tent stood Ina, wearing sandals, a sarong draped loosely around her waist, her hair in a carefree bun – ready for the day.

"Oh, shut up, Bruce! Your welding mask has fallen over your eyes," Ina said as she took her place on the back of the Bedford.

Bruce never drank again.

Landmine

We were still sitting there when the child stepped on the land-mine. With an earth-shattering roar her leg was torn off and her belly ripped open.

It was early morning when Leon van Kraaienberg and I took off from Nelspruit in the Jet Bell Ranger. He, an experienced chopper pilot, and I, commissioned by the Mozambican government to determine if there were any buffalo and elephant left in the northern provinces of Niassa, Cabo del Gado and Tete. It was a long way to fly. Right across Zimbabwe and Malawi, and then on to the Ruvuma River, which forms the border between Mozambique and Tanzania.

Actually I was lucky, for we were looking at fifteen hours in the air, while a ground crew with Lampies and Arnold behind the wheel was tackling this section of Africa overland. They were hoping to be at the rendezvous on the banks of the Lugenda River in five days' time.

The exercise cost a great deal of money. For every hour that the engines were running, we had to fork out two thousand rand – not to mention the cost of the ground crew and other logistical expenses. The chopper was loaded with plastic fuel cans, because the distances were too great to reach the refuelling points on normal tanks. I realised we were flying in a potential bomb, but I put my faith in Leon, who came very highly recommended.

We flew over Africa at a height of five hundred feet. It was an incredible experience to see the world from that perspective. At Punda Maria – in the north of the Kruger Park – we roused a herd of elephant. I secretly hoped that we would also see it happen further north. Or had the terrible war in Mozambique resulted in all game being decimated in a bid to survive? Fortunately a war in that region had held no real strategic military advantage – which was why the Mozambicans had asked us to investigate.

Somewhere on a rocky hill in the middle of Zimbabwe the helicopter touched down and we refuelled from the cans. We had unlawfully set foot on foreign soil. I used the opportunity to light my pipe. A long trip like this one could get boring, and Leon and I had already spoken at length about our families, our pasts and our futures.

From the air the destruction of the African bush was apparent. The local farmers make use of the traditional "slash and burn" method, where the bush is chopped down, set alight and the ashes ploughed in as fertiliser – for a single crop and for only one season. Then they move on. Leon told me about his second wife and their child back home.

At one stage we flew across Lake Malawi. It is a huge expanse of water. An anxious thought crossed my mind: If this flying machine should crash here, how the hell would we come out alive? It would sink like a stone and we would not be able to get out from under the rotors. Not until the water had forced them to a standstill. What was more, I had never exactly been Mark Spitz. Leon told me his wish was that if he were to die, it would be in a helicopter!

Once everyone had arrived at the rendezvous, we set to work. The scenery was incredible, with mahobohobo veld as far as the eye could see. Scattered rocky inselbergs towering over the surrounding landscape. The Ruvuma River with its masses of water and countless herds of elephant, buffalo and Lichtenstein's hartebeest! We saw sable antelope and kudu. Clearly the war had not wreaked complete havoc here.

A Pomzet antipersonnel mine is a terrible thing. Mind you, it merely does what is expected of it, namely to bugger up the person who steps on it in such a way that it costs a great deal of money, effort and logistics to evacuate him – or her – and to put the person together again. If it happens to a soldier, he is usually out of the game of war permanently. The state is obliged to supply him with a medical pension and to support and look after him, an invalid for the rest of his life. Thus the main aim of a Pomzet is to force the enemy to its knees economically.

By the time we reached the child, her terrified, screaming little friends were crowding around her. A landmine casualty is *really* bad. I'd rather not go into detail. Sometimes the victim simply dies of shock.

The other children were ushered away and, ignoring the threat of Aids, we began to rip up cloth for bandages. We all had basic first-aid knowledge and we managed to stop the bleeding. The little body was rigid with shock and the eyes were white in the face. I realised that the child was not going to survive if she wasn't evacuated to receive proper medical care.

We looked at each other. The child was dying under our hands. Some distance away stood the chopper . . . It was a nine-hour flight to Maputo – it would cost thirty-six thousand rand, not to mention the time lost.

Before anyone could say a word, a black woman came charging through the bush.

She didn't cry. She didn't scream. The anger in her eyes seemed to supplant all emotion. She clutched the child to her breast, looked at us as if she wanted to say, "Leave my child alone, you bastards," and walked back into the bush, carrying the broken little body.

P.S. Two months later Leon died in a car crash somewhere between Nelspruit and Watervalboven. The rescue helicopter could not evacuate him.

Sangoma

The air conditioning in the departure hall of the Windhoek airport was nothing to write home about. And it was sizzling. There wasn't even a proper bar – just a Coca Cola fridge against one wall, stocked with lukewarm beer. I sat in the smokers' section, slurping at a Windhoek Lager and drawing on a cigarette.

Duty-free at any international airport is just a gimmick. Everything is more expensive, in my opinion, and it's all part of a devious plot to con the tourists out of the last of their currency. Windhoek didn't have much on offer, however. Except for the ubiquitous perfume and liquor, there was a lone novelties stand, attempting to peddle African souvenirs. Now, if there's one thing I have learned during my travels, it is to distinguish between the real thing and a fake article, destined for the tourist market. En route to the beer, I recognised the mass-produced goods of Kenya, Malawi and Zimbabwe – nothing uniquely Namibian. The shop assistant was a Vambo woman, neatly clad in khaki. But there were no interested buyers.

My flight back to the Republic was still a half-hour away and I fetched myself another lukewarm beer. Among the usual crap on display, I had noticed a few exceptional items – small clay passport masks from Gabon and the Cameroon in West Africa. The little masks fit in the palm of your hand and in the old days served to identify the bearer when people moved from one area to another.

African art has its own particular attraction. Some like it, others don't, but to distinguish a fake from the real thing you need a little knowledge. Not all ethnic groups concentrate on creative art, but certain items remain distinctive. In Zimbabwe the Shona make the most beautiful soapstone sculptures. Fertility dolls are typical of Kenya. The Maconde statues, depicting an entire community and made from a single piece of wood, are endemic to Tanzania. The bronze castings from Mali are remarkable, as are the colourful figurines from the Côte d'Ivoire. Coin-studded masks usually come from Nigeria, just as heads carved out of hard ebony are typically Zambian. Handwoven, brightly coloured fabrics from Burkina Faso compete with mud-painted cloths from the Korogo in the Ivory Coast and batik from Zimbabwe.

"Are you a sangoma?" the lady at the stall asked, noticing my collection of copper and leather bracelets.

It was a loaded question – especially if I chose to answer truthfully.

The blacks in suburban Pretoria had adopted me as their sangoma. I – who shopped at the supermarket in bare feet and kikoi, who dropped off a crate of beer at the garage at Christmas time and walked in the Irene koppies in the afternoons for exercise, with my walking stick and backpack, passing illegal shebeens on my way. "Induku" they called me – "kierie", or "walking stick".

I usually protested: "No, but . . ." For I knew this was a domain better avoided by the uninformed. But the displaced person needs a sympathetic ear and I began to listen. The problems were always the same:

"My husband is cheating on me."

"I can't survive on my wages."

"I'm going to court tomorrow."

"I've got a pain just here . . ."

"I'm looking for a job."

My "consultation room" was furnished with Malawian chairs, carved from a single piece of wood, and numerous statues and masks from all over Africa. During "consultations" a big fire blazed at our feet, underneath a Karoo thorn that had been specially planted in suburbia. Advice was meted out carefully – the logical Western kind. Not once did I resort to traditional cult practices. I was never more than the listener and the induna, who offered advice based on his own experience. But it must have worked, because there was never a lack of callers.

"I don't throw dolos and I don't dance, but what's the matter?" I once again ventured into the unknown.

"I'm looking for a job. I only help out here at the stall. Please help me," said the woman.

I gave her a Western reply: "If you sell a lot of things and make a lot of money for the owner, he will think: 'Perhaps I should keep this girl.'"

"But no one buys anything! I have been here all day. People just walk past and get on their planes."

The announcement came: "Passengers on flight 832 to Johannesburg are requested to go on board." I got up, relieved, and laid a hand on her shoulder. "You'll see," I said as I left.

I settled into my seat, fastened my seatbelt and got ready for the two-hour flight. Suddenly there was another announcement: "One of our in-flight attendants has been taken ill. We are waiting for a replacement from Windhoek. The flight has been delayed for an hour. Passengers may return to the departure hall to stretch their legs."

I was the first one out. The woman at the stall looked at me, surprised, as I passed her on my way to the smokers' section. "We've been delayed," I answered her unspoken question.

"Surely a sangoma can make the plane fly?"

I smiled and shook my head. The little passport masks caught my eye again and I bought one. That was the signal for the rest of the passengers to descend on the kiosk. And every time she put a gift into a paper bag, her eyes found mine, as I sat sipping at a lukewarm beer. And she gave me a broad smile.

A lucky man

It was noon in the Little Karoo and sweltering. The Barrydale was as closed as the eye of the proverbial clay ox. I had been warned: "Philip will open only if he feels like it, or if he likes you."

I leaned against the doorbell. It rang once, twice, three times. Dimly I heard footsteps.

A chink through which an eye peered.

"Yes?"

"I would like to take a little something – do you have a bar?"

The door was opened slightly wider.

"I have a helluva hangover – I partied last night, right here in my own hotel," a voice came from inside and the eye looked me up and down. Silence. "OK, come inside."

And I stepped into another world . . . I'm not an interior decorator, so I don't know how to describe the scene I was confronted with. I don't know if terms like "decadent", "kitsch", "overpowering", "mid-nineteenth century France", "Moulin Rouge", "riot of colour" or "onslaught on the senses" would be any use. I stood amazed. Yet everything made sense. Heavy dark velvet, colourful cushions, life-sized murals, statues and flower arrangements, everything as if it were *meant* to be like that.

"The bar is around the corner. I'm busy. Go pour yourself a shot. I'll be right there," he said, disappearing among the labyrinth of objects.

I had thankfully never encountered anything like this before, I realised as I seated myself at the counter. Oude Meester transformed into a Toulouse-Lautrec South Sea Islands girl, deep-cushioned sofas alternated with church pews, old B-movie posters from the beginning of the previous century – all of it left me staring in open-mouthed wonder.

While I was pouring a drink, a stern Tannie Mo entered with Philip in tow like a naughty little boy.

"She stops me from spending my entire profit on booze – she's been a bar lady for thirteen years," he said laconically, helping himself to a cold beer.

I made enquiries. He had bought the hotel about two years before in a crazy moment of truth; at the time he had been the owner of the well-known Jaart and Boerebar in Pretoria. "I was doing well there, but I couldn't stand myself. *Here* I met Philip Uys and made my dream come true: the dream of helping myself to liquor and cigarettes, in any quantity and as often as I like."

We drank deeply. I asked about staff, visitors and tourists.

"It's just Tannie Mo, Maureen in the kitchen, and me. We get only the occasional visitor. Oh yes, and then there are the Ayleward spinsters, of course." He took another sip.

"The Ayleward spinsters?" I asked.

"Yes, they served as nurses in the War, and afterwards their father bought them this little hotel. One played the organ and the other one counted the cash. They cooked for weary travellers, poured drinks, bestowed other favours and provided for various needs. They still wander around late at night, taking care of weary travellers," he said, glancing sanctimoniously at the ceiling. "I am at peace – I have no money, no lover – I can do as I please, and then I have the Ayleward sisters as well . . ."

I decided to book into the hotel for the night and was given the Purple Room. I also planned to visit Ronnie that night.

"Make yourself at home. I'll leave the kitchen door open," were Philip's words of farewell.

That night I partied up a storm with Ronnie and Ludwig in their Sex Shop. It was after the witching hour when I pushed open the kitchen door of The Barrydale quietly . . .

A candle flickered and died as two beautiful girls in white flannel nightgowns helped me carefully up the stairs.

A father

"To be a parent isn't always easy," my mother used to say. At this point, as I try to play the role myself, I realise it is true. I do think, however, that it was more difficult to be a father in earlier days. A father was never supposed to show his feelings, he certainly couldn't cry. His role was that of material provider. As long as he was strong all would be well with everyone. It was the norm. Today I know that all fathers want to safeguard their children from the onslaughts of life in their own way.

My father had four children. As a child on the West Coast, I remember my father with his backpack, leading us up Binnekopberg or Malgaskop on a Friday evening after work. The backpack was stocked with chops, sausages and bread rolls. And stories. As the sun set across Danger Bay, we listened, enthralled.

The story of the day Van Riet Reitz and he took off in their homemade tomato box airplane, and met their match in the Drakensberg. Of the time he was a Stormtrooper in the Ossewa Brandwag, and cycled all around Church Square, fleeing from the police and shouting "Down with Britain!" The story of the bloodstain, of Andreas Hofer, the Tyrolean freedom fighter, and of Jopie Fourie. He told us about heroes.

My father didn't have a father. His own father died when he was three months old. I came to understand that his had been a solitary path, with one resolve: "My children will always have a father." And we *did* have one.

Petty Officer Chappie Snyman of *SAS Saldanha* also had four children. Three girls and Tjaart, who was my age. I remember Tjaart as a boy who could run – which was more or less the only form of athletics we West Coast children were able to take part in. Duwweltjies and all. You just dragged your feet across the sand at the start. Of javelin and pole vault we would only learn many years later.

Rugged sailor that Chappie was, it was important to him that young people should be exposed to the joys of nature and the outdoor life. Introduce them to a different form of pleasure, and the "evils" of LM Radio or secret smoking wouldn't be an option, he had possibly thought. We children had to address him as "Petty Officer". I imagine his own children had a hard life, judging by Tjaart, who regularly came to school with red eyes and a matching red backside. Chappie himself was a man of few words. I don't know whether he had a father.

It was he who took us children, each with his own little backpack, to Donkergat by boat. From there we walked to Saldanha by way of the Langebaan lagoon, with Chappie leading us military style. One night, in pouring rain, we sought shelter in Lord Charles Somerset's dilapidated farmstead, Geelbek. We "commandeered" an ostrich egg at Oesterwal and cooked breakfast on the beach. In his own way he opened up another part of life for us children, though at home we still secretly listened to LM Radio.

My father, the eternal soldier and romantic, left Saldanha, and we moved to the Transvaal, where he bought us a piece of Bushveld. As a government official on a monthly salary, it could not have been easy, I realise today. But in the bush he made the world an even bigger place for us. I remember a birthday when he laid ambushes for my friends and me with 303 and blank cartridges and afterwards told us tales of peace.

Two years after we had left Saldanha, we opened the Sunday paper one morning. The headlines shouted: PETTY OFFICER WIPES OUT FAMILY!

Every man tries in his own way . . .

The women of Skardu

"Why are you going there?" our wives asked.

"It's the mountain peaks, those high ones with ice and snow and glaciers," we tried to explain.

"But you know bugger all about snow, and the little that you know is dangerous," they retorted.

"Ag, it's just to get away from you women." Chauvinistic to the end, we departed . . .

Four of us were travelling to Pakistan. The plan was to tackle the glaciers of the Karakoram mountain range, home to the second highest mountain in the world, K2, deep in the Northern Province of Baltistan. It is very dangerous, we were told. Not only the mountains, but Pakistan per se. There are quite a few ways of losing your money – and your life.

Friendly curio sellers, beggars, taxi drivers, prospective "guides", all try to strip the unwary tourist of his cash. Pickpocketing and theft have been honed to a fine art. "Never leave your possessions unattended," said those in the know. And the field in which Pakistan seems to surpass most other places in the world . . . the cold calculated art of kidnapping and blackmail. You should also try to avoid landing in the middle of an ethnic struggle such as Pakistan and India's Kashmir mess. And if none of the preceding happens to you, you are almost certain to die in a motor accident or be knocked to hell and gone by a car.

The Islamic Republic of Pakistan is, as its name says, a Muslim country and Islamic laws are enforced by government. In 1977 alcohol was banned completely. The institution of the Hudood ordinance in 1984 made specific Shariah Islamic codes law. Under Shariah law, theft is punished with amputation, immorality with stoning and blasphemy against Mohammed with death.

Our reception in Islamabad was friendly. Sayd, the tour guide, invited us to his home and we sat down for a meal. Though he told us he had six daughters, only men were seated at the carefully laid table. From a kitchen somewhere at the back I heard sounds of activity. A while later the door opened and a beautiful young woman entered the dining room with lowered head. I greeted, but she pretended that I did not exist.

"My eldest daughter. She's married, but lives with me," Sayd remarked in passing.

But we were there for the mountains and soon we were in a bus, racing along the Karakoram highway to the north. The word "highway" must not be misunderstood. Though the road happens to be tarred, it is so narrow that two vehicles can barely squeeze past each other. To make it worse, the road winds its way up dizzying heights, with the Indus River furiously carving its way to the sea far below. Round every bend death stared us in the face, especially when a truck or some similar large vehicle came from the front. Then there was much hooting and gesticulating, and with one wheel hovering over the sheer drop, the drivers shaved past each other at high speed.

It's strange how you think of your family when you look into the hollow eyes of death. We *had* said we wanted to get away from our wives, and look at us now. Suddenly I realised I yet had to lay eyes on a Pakistani woman (with the exception of the brief glimpse of Sayd's daughter).

Pakistan is the ninth or tenth most densely populated country in the world. It is home to about 146 million people, though no truly successful census has been taken since 1981. More than half the people are younger than 15. In 1998 the average Pakistani had a life expectancy of about 55 and, strangely enough, it is lower for women than for men. (This applies to only three other countries – India, Bangladesh and Nepal.)

We spent two nerve-shattering days on the road. At last we reached Skardu, the capital of Baltistan. Here we were to meet the guides and bearers who would be accompanying us on our glacier adventure. It was afternoon, and we went to the bazaar to exchange our American dollars for rupees.

The place looked like any busy third world village, teeming dustily with people. They sat around lazily, peering at passers-by. Did I say "people"? I meant *men*, for in the entire bustling place

87

there was not a single woman in sight. Shop owners, officials, clients, passers-by, vagrants, inquisitive spectators . . . all men.

Suddenly I remembered two bits of information. We had been warned never to photograph a woman or make any eye contact at all, for it could be taken as an insult. I realised, however, that we would be sticking to the rules anyway, for clearly we were never going to lay eyes on that species of the Pakistani population.

I bought myself a Pakistani outfit, consisting of a long flowing robe, and over a bottle of cool drink we met Mohammed Kahn, our guide. He filled us in.

The family is the most important social structure in Pakistan. Neither race nor nationality nor social class nor wealth is as important as the family, or "clan". The system is strongly patriarchal. Women are seen as inferior to men but at the same time as very valuable. They are mothers and housekeepers, and you protect them with your life.

According to the Muslim tradition, women are kept away from all men outside the family circle after puberty. When they go out, they are cloaked from head to toe in a burqa, a tent-like dress.

Marriages are usually arranged for girls during their teenage years, and traditionally they marry a second cousin on their fathers' side. It is also expected of a girl to provide an enormous dowry, which can sometimes plunge her entire family into bankruptcy. The result is that a baby girl is simply not as welcome as a baby boy.

Our travels took us further into the rugged mountains of the Karakoram. The road was untarred and we headed up the cliffs in four-wheel drive. The nightmare became even worse. Rockfalls and chunks of road simply breaking away were an imminent danger. We were travelling in small Jeeps, and once inside the contraption, there was no escape. The road was so narrow that, if you got out on the side of the abyss, you would take a fall of hundreds of metres. On the other side you were pressed up against the cliffs and it was simply impossible to get out.

I began to wonder if I should not have stayed at home with my dear wife after all.

I remembered reading that, according to Amnesty International, there are hundreds of Pakistani women in jail under the Zina ordinance at any given time. This ordinance decrees that sex outside of matrimony is punishable. Pregnancy outside of marriage is evidence of adultery; the possibility of rape is not readily considered. A man can be accused of adultery only if there were several witnesses. There must also be at least four male witnesses before a man can be charged with rape; this means that a rape victim is often convicted of adultery and the rapist gets off scot-free. There is no penalty for rape within marriage.

Pakistani courts have sent women who dared to get married against their fathers' will back to their parents' home. Abused wives are summarily sent home by the police. According to a 1996 report by the Human Rights Commission of Pakistan, married women are sometimes killed by relatives in disputes about dowries. In most cases they are burned to death . . . in what is reported as kitchen accidents.

At a military control point somewhere in Kashmir we were stopped. The men in khaki uniforms seemed nervous and ordered us to get out. No one could speak English and they snapped at us in Urdu. Things were not looking good. In Africa it always helps if you say "Bafana Bafana" or "Mandela". I knew it was not going to work here, but to alleviate the tension I tried:

"Cricket," I said and hit an imaginary four.

"Hansie Cronjé, Imran Khan," I tried again, and came up with some bowling action.

It helped bugger all.

A stern lieutenant, his chest covered with medals, made a bee-line for me. He took out an Indian magazine with a full-page photograph of a pretty (fully clothed) woman.

"Have you got sexy magazine?" he asked, tapping on the photograph with his finger.

And I thought to myself: You bastards.

The world was sleeping . . .

The wind tugged violently at the tent, which was squatly trying to stand its ground. Swaddled snugly in my sleeping bag, I realised we were being snowed in here on the Biafo glacier. At 4 000 metres, the air was thin. Like often before, I wondered why on earth I found myself in a situation like this – civilisation, with its luxuries and delicacies, was much safer, after all. At that moment I would have given anything for a fire in the hearth and some red wine . . .

The climb up to that point had been extremely difficult – up and down over moraine debris and rock, higher and higher into the thin air.

A glacier has its own soul. It is alive. Chasms yawning for miles into its heart. Rocks letting go and crashing down. Scree starting to shift, unprovoked, and phalanxes of rock suddenly collapsing. And all the time the ice is moving, growling, from the depth of its stomach.

You realise you're not really welcome – man has no place here. But it is beautiful: the Karakoram peaks towering a further 3 000 metres into the air on either side; icebergs, with glaciers like icing sugar all the way down to the Biafo, which, in combination with the Hispar, forms the longest glacier outside the polar regions.

The Pakistani guides and bearers from Baltistan, on the border of Kashmir, hauled 35-kg loads over relentless terrain without respite. We had known bearers before – Nepalese Sherpas and Swahili Tanzanians – but these hardy mountain men astonished us. With vacant expressions, they sidestepped loose stones and crevices and toiled up the heights.

My tent began to wobble under the weight of the snow. From the inside I knocked against the canvas to shake off the snow. Breathless, I lay back down. It was bitterly cold; my breath was condensing and dripping down icily. To stop myself from freezing, I hummed a tune by the Radiators: "Fok . . . maar dis warm in Johannesburg" – Fuck . . . it's hot in Johannesburg.

The Karakoram range lies slightly behind the Himalayas. K2,

known as the Savage Mountain, is the second highest mountain in the world, where more climbers have died than on any other peak except Nanga Parbat, the Killer Mountain, also in Pakistan. The range is bordered by Afghanistan, Pakistan, China and India and contains four of the world's fourteen 8 000-metre peaks. We were on our way to Snow Lake – at 5 000 metres according to some people one of the most beautiful places in the world. Few people ever get to see it, because of the hazardous glacier route and the lack of oxygen at that height . . .

Four of us were sharing this adventure. At the moment each was alone in his tent, occupied by his own thoughts. I knew that the question "What the hell am I doing here?" was going through all our minds. Surely it would be much more agreeable to sit snugly sheltered in our skyscraper offices or spend time around the kitchen table with our families?

Two days ago our progress had been slow. We had to search for alternate routes around the yawning crevasses. These ice-blue cracks reaching into the unfathomable depths are truly frightening. One false step or slip on the ice and you're done for. At one point I was walking alone – the guides in front and the bearers at the back obscured by waves of ice. I was obliged to find my own way and I was gripped by a terrible loneliness. Once again I was filled with admiration for men like Amundsen, Robert Scott and Fiennes, who had ventured blindly into unknown polar regions.

We left the glacier and struggled to the side across boulders and scree before tackling a steep slope. It drained the last of our energy. There was no air, and it was onward and upward by fits and starts. Then we encountered a fierce wind on an exposed cliffside that towered 100 metres into the sky. I nearly soiled myself when the wind slammed my backpack against the rock face and my ice pick almost drove me over the edge and into the depths . . .

Everyone has an excuse for why he is doing what might not be generally acceptable. It was Mallory who had said we climb mountains because they are there. The smoker might say:

"There's only one road to a man's lungs and it should be tarred." Or the excessive drinker might remark: "Alcohol is evil, so I have to finish it all before my kids grow up." But one shouldn't *have* to explain, as friend Kalie once quoted somebody. If you don't know, you won't understand, and if you had known, you wouldn't have asked.

Yesterday morning light snow began to fall and it was lying ankle-deep as we moved out across the glacier. The glacier itself looked different: a broad, snow-white runway, extending for kilometres. No crevasses in sight. I noticed that Mohammed, our guide, was looking wild-eyed as he spoke urgently to his assistant guides and bearers. We strung up the slope in a long line, with Mahmud, one of the assistant guides, darting ahead, finding a safe route.

From a distance a mound of snow came rolling in our direction. I realised that these people were economically dependent on the success of the expedition. They were even prepared to lay down their lives on this treacherous snow-covered glacier. I also realised that, with the crevasses covered by snow, no one was certain of his life. Had we passed the point of no return?

The thought that it was going to be a long night brought me back to the present. The cold was creeping up on us. What did tomorrow hold? I thought of my family and knew that they, at least, were safe and warm. Here we were, fearing that we might not come out of here alive, and the rest of the world – totally unaware of our situation – was going about its usual business.

I looked at my watch . . . it was 03:45 . . . it was 11 September 2001 and the world was sleeping.

Wealth

The heat was sweltering and the sun scorching. If I didn't find water immediately, I was going to die. Was history repeating itself? How could I have been so stupid? Pinkie had said the Hunsberg wasn't to be trifled with. It wasn't for nothing that, in the early 1900s, the German Schutztruppen of South-West Africa had refused to go there, giving it a wide berth.

Surely Pinkie's directions had been clear enough, or had his memory failed him? It had been nearly fifty years since he was last here, after all. You cross the Fish River at the Kochas drift – turn left across the Asbos plain, passing along the foot of Spieël-berg – go up along the Konkiep, past Bitterwater to Mara. Leave the bakkie there and continue on foot, following the tributary of the Naub and climbing in the direction of Hohenzollern peak. It was about a five-hour hike – that was all he had remembered.

Actually these mountains were terrifying. Rock and stones everywhere, with scattered milk bushes and occasionally a lone quiver tree. It looked as if the mountain had been stripped of its skin, with the sun burning itself to a frazzle on the cliffs. Five hours, my arse! Or was I lost? My water was finished – everything began to look the same to me. The iron ore in the rocks caused my compass to spin randomly. Please don't let it be far!

In the bar at Maltahöhe he had told me his story. As a child he had tended sheep in these parts. As a young man he had worked in the mines at Tsumeb – and had lost his little finger in a rock-fall. Hence the nickname, Pinkie. He was a wanderer and an adventurer, and South-West was his first love. He knew the land like the back of his hand.

"In the forties a story did the rounds that there are unimaginable riches hidden in the Hunsberg. There was talk of diamond lodes that are clearly visible. But it was only with the advent of aerial photography that those terrifying mountains were charted. Those who ventured there never returned.

"It's everyone's dream, treasure like that," Pinkie continued. "I began to ask around and one day I came across an old prospector who confirmed the story. He gave me vague directions but added that no treasure was worth the peril of setting foot in those mountains."

We drank another pampelmoes and chased it with a beer.

"Armed with a canteen of water, a 303 and the old man's directions, I went into the mountains. And sure enough, in a ravine somewhere near the Hohenzollern peak, I saw them. Diamonds wherever you looked, embedded in iron ore. I was overwhelmed but I realised not even with a chisel would I be able to pry the stuff loose."

The pampelmoeses followed one another in quick succession.

"For hours I stared at the unbelievable sight. Immeasurable wealth, but not meant for me. When at last I turned and left, I no longer knew where I was. I got so lost in those mountains that I thought I would never see another living soul. An old Nama picked me up for dead at Namuskluft three days later – in my near-dead state I made a promise to the Lord that I would never return."

I began to hallucinate. Was this wilderness swallowing me? I scrambled up a slope – from up there everything looked even more similar. Something told me to turn around – but where to? Water? And I had always thought I knew how to survive in the wilderness.

You have to be calm now, I told myself. I would have to get out under my own steam, for no one was going to come looking for me. I moved into the shade of an overhanging rock. Keep your wits about you, Boetie, I thought, you're in deep shit.

The most important thing was water. The sun had already passed its zenith. I had to find a direction to follow and wait for the sun to lose its sting. With my eyes closed, I lay thinking of treasure and riches. Material things have never held any special appeal for me. All right, I need a bakkie and enough money for fuel and . . . My wealth lies in experience, in memories and what is in my heart. My treasure chest is nature and Africa is

96

my continent. But now I was lying here, facing the possibility of never getting out again, purely because I had gone in search of diamonds.

My mouth was extremely dry by now, my tongue sticking to my palate. Your average man can survive four minutes without air, four days without water and forty days without food. Air there was enough of, so I had four days to get out.

Late afternoon – I got to my feet and set off in an easterly direction. To the east lay the Fish River and to the west the Skeleton Coast. I struggled along a dry river bed. The going was tough, across boulders and through deep sand, but I knew any river running east should spit me out in the Fish River – everything depended on how long it would take.

Suddenly I noticed animal tracks in the sand – they appeared to belong to mountain zebra. The Hartmann's mountain zebra is found only in Namibia and cannot go without water like the gemsbok. It likes to drink in the late afternoon – there should therefore be water around here somewhere. Hastily I followed the tracks, and soon I came across fresh dung!

As I rounded a bend in the river bed, I was faced by a sharp decline and about a hundred metres further – to be sure, there they stood in the early twilight! And under an overhanging rock there was a pool of water!

But something wasn't right – was I still hallucinating? I could swear the creatures standing in front of me were not mountain zebra after all. They looked like zebra, but the distinctive stripes were missing from their haunches.

My foot dislodged a stone – the heads of the small herd jerked up as one, and, whinnying, they vanished along the river bed.

Had my eyes deceived me? Could it really be? Had I just witnessed the last herd of the extinct quagga, here in the uninhabitable Hunsberg . . .?

Flotsam

She is neatly dressed in black. The tailored suit and high heels look out of place on the quay in the harbour of Dakar. I am sitting at a watering hole, a cold Flag beer in my hand. The sun is melting into the oily bay. To my left Senegalese fishermen are washing their catch in the shallows. A big, sturdy boatsman unceremoniously pisses like a fountain.

She is the first white girl I have seen the past few days and, what is more, she is pretty. I notice the expensive jewellery as she starts walking in my direction, her handbag swinging . . .

The gleaming, jingling bodies around me are dancing with increasing fervour to the rhythm of the salsa. The dive here in Maputo harbour is packed. The music, though ear-splitting, is also captivating. Dirty and bedraggled, I am squashed into a corner, drinking a rot-gut rum and Cola. Except for the large, fair-haired German beside me, festooned with gold chains and sporting a Rolex, I seem to be the only European present. The rest vary between darkest African, Mulatto and Creole.

It seems as if the music has taken possession of the people. From the corner of my eye I notice a tall, slim descendant of the Portuguese colonialists dancing voluptuously in my direction . . .

We find ourselves somewhere in the Casablanca medina, looking for a place to sleep. Dense hashish clouds hang in the air as the door of the small house is opened for the Swiss and me. Mattresses lie on the floor of the entrance hall.

The old woman pulls deeply and obliviously at the bubbling pipe. A girl comes floating along, clad in kaftan and veil. Her deep-brown eyes questioning. Looking for overnight accommodation? The eyes brighten as she sizes us up.

It is the only private room. I test the bed. It gives way like a hammock, leaving my arse hovering just above the ground, but at least the bed is clean. Affirmative. "Combien?" – How much? – asks the Swiss from behind me. And the girl from the thousand and one Arabian nights steps closer . . .

It is pumpkin hour. My drinking partner is well and truly smashed. A sailor, tattooed, who missed the last ferry to his ship in the Durban harbour. Partly so that I won't be stuck with him, I have dragged him along to the quay.

Suddenly from a dark alley: "Oom, vir vyftig rand sal ek doen net wat julle vra" – For fifty rand I'll do whatever you ask.

The Afrikaans gives me a jolt – she is barely fourteen, her lips painted coquettishly red. Clumsily she advances on me . . .

On the beach. There are two of them, heading straight for us. The damp firewood smokes and sputters while I'm trying to braai some meat. My guest is the Indian skipper of a ferry in Dar es Salaam.

The careless, dishevelled appearance of the girls spells "overlander", a particular species of traveller in Africa. They join us: "How do we get to Zanzibar?"

I know, for my clients left on the ferry that morning and I look at my guest enquiringly. "How much?"

Every port has its own despair. Dakar, with the adventure of savage love; Maputo, where the rich promise an escape from poverty; Casablanca, and the hope of exchanging Africa for Europe; Durban, where a sailor promises a passage to better horizons and Dar es Salaam, where the tariff for a new adventure is negotiable.

And I remain on the outside, looking in.

Bread on the water

The station at Bamako was rank. Rank with the smell of bananas and cabbage, stinking dead chickens, piss, human sweat and excrement. It was humidly hot. The heavy, stifling air enveloped me. I was pouring with sweat and felt as sticky and filthy as the station itself.

My destination was Dakar, Senegal. I had been told by the locals here in the capital of Mali that I would have to stand in line for days if I wanted a place on the weekly train. I was not the only one – the queue went on and on. It seemed that most people had been in line for longer than the recommended four days. Nothing could make them give up their places – brightly clad women simply raised their dresses and let go right where they stood in line. The chickens, intended for hungry children somewhere along the tracks, were dead – but they were food. Children were crying, women were scolding and men protested loudly if any bugger tried to jump the queue. I was struck by the total desperation.

I was the only white person. My French was dodgy. My backpack and I went meekly to the back of the queue . . .

"Sir, I can help you?" I was startled by the English.

"How?"

"I can get you a first-class ticket. Come back in four days' time and everything will be organised."

Oh, fuck, another scam, I thought, despondent and sweating, but at least it was better than four days in a queue.

"How much commission?" I asked.

"Sir, I'm Sergeant Husaka from Nigeria. I was part of the last unsuccessful military coup and I'm in Mali illegally. I need money to lie low – you decide."

And I looked at him and recognised the soldier in his eyes. And I told him about South Africa and my own war and my rank and I gave him my trust and my train fare and I left.

The Bamako-Dakar train was the only one still running in those parts of West Africa and only just. The railway line was sinking away and maintenance no longer existed. However, it was the only form of transport through swamp and savannah. The real first class was on the roof, I had heard, because at least there was air to breathe and you were able to jump if the train derailed . . .

Four days later I was back at the station at dusk, sticky and sweaty and dragging my heavy backpack. The people were still queuing and it didn't look as if the ticket office had opened at all. Was I imagining it, or did I recognise that elegant woman with the brightly coloured headdress?

No, I thought, I had backed the wrong horse here. Despondently I sat down on my backpack at the back of the queue. The train was supposed to leave in two hours' time and I didn't have a ticket.

"Captain, Sir, good evening," I heard, and in front of me stood Sergeant Husaka. "Please join me. Your ticket is ready."

We struggled through the masses to the platform and the waiting train. "Battered" was not an adequate description. "Busted", perhaps, or "unserviceable", or "fucked up", but at the front an engine was steaming.

"First class," said the sergeant and pointed at a carriage that still had windows. He handed me a ticket, a packet of ice to cool me down and a surreptitious twist of weed for the journey. We put my backpack in one of the compartments and stood talking on the platform.

He told me of the problems in his country. Of corruption and treachery. Of their failed rebellion, of his futureless life. Of being on the run and having to leave his wife and children behind. I told him about Mandela and Bafana Bafana and the rainbow Utopia in the distant south. An African with a white skin was a problematic concept for him, but I told him about the Maburu, the white tribe of Africa. And when the train whistled, I handed a generous commission, a small flag of the Republic and my home address to the soldier whose word was his bond.

When the train lurched and pulled away, a swarm of vampire bats the size of vultures burst from the trees around the station and flew, shrieking, in the direction of the full moon . . .

My travel guide said I was in for a 36-hour journey, so I made my way through the crowded corridor to my compartment. There were six of us in a four-berth cubicle. My fellow travellers sat packed like sardines in a tin, silently staring at one another. I wormed myself in and sat staring too. I didn't understand their language anyway and I was finding it difficult to breathe. The window was shut. The next 36 hours were going to be hell. To break the deadly silence I tried to introduce myself in English. A thin Arab understood and said he was a government man from Mauritania. In French he explained to the others who I was. Our fellow travellers were two Malians on their way to Dakar for a business transaction. The other two were Senegalese; one was a dentist, the other a merchant. Our "conversation" dried up.

My companions were settling in to spend the night sleeping in their seats. The Senegalese dentist took off his shoes and, fuck, his feet were in a sorry state. They were covered with open, inflamed sores and looked extremely painful – I had my doubts about his medical background. I couldn't bear his obvious pain and discomfort and took my first-aid kit from my backpack. I doused the sores with Merthiolate and gave him a painkiller. There was a grateful smile in his eyes as I turned to leave – I wasn't going to get any sleep here; I would rather stand in the corridor.

I found a spot on the steps in the open door and, while the train was speeding through the jungle, I tried to doze. Sometime in the early hours I woke as a man bent over me in the dark. It was the dentist, offering me a can of cool drink and gesticulating to inquire after my wellbeing.

Bread on the water, I thought.

First light found me still on the steps. I was dirtier than ever, and the grass seeds that had blown in through the door were clinging to my clothes and hair. I tried the toilet, but two young goats bleated a greeting when I wanted to take a leak. They were tied to the towel rail. The other toilet was chock-a-block with bags of salt, mealie meal and sugar, and I realised I was destined to hold it in for 36 hours.

At the border town Kayes I rushed to the police station to check out of Mali. No one could tell me how long the train would be standing there. At Kadira on the Senegalese side all non-Senegalese and Malians were gathered in a group and marched to the police station under escort. The Mauritanian was with me. The rest turned out to be from Burkino Faso and Nigeria. The Mauritanian got his stamp, two Nigerians were arrested and my passport was scrutinised by officials.

I became anxious. What now? I looked around, bewildered. From whence cometh my help? Under a tree outside the police station I spotted the Senegalese dentist, watching . . . Bread on the water . . .

I remained on the steps for the rest of our journey, gazing in wonder at the African bush. The baobabs were bigger than those in the Messina district. The savannah and thorn trees were as beautiful as they were near Otjiwarongo, but nowhere was there any sign of wildlife. This is elephant and buffalo country, I thought. Though I wondered, I actually *knew* what had happened to them.

Back in my office in Pretoria, I received a letter. It was a short one.

Captain Sir,
They have arrested me. I'm in jail in Bamako, the address is:
Central Jail Bamako
Private Bag X17
Bamako
Mali
Yours truly,
Sergeant Hosea Husaka

Bread on the water, I thought, and began to write a letter to Joe Modise, Minister of Defence.

It's late, but my future is beckoning

It was late when Pop, Dog and I struggled through Kimberley. The bakkie was loaded. We were moving to the Western Cape. Life was changing. I had pulled up my roots and after thirty years I was returning to my place of origin. What did the future hold for me?

Dog was an Airedale, from a litter of ten. He'd found a new owner in Claremont. I have never been fond of domestic animals. They're a nuisance and restrict one's freedom of movement. And every so often you step in a pile of dogshit. But this nameless dog had grown on me after a day on the road. He didn't puke, shit or climb all over the car. He lay calmly and looked at me, wide-eyed. Now and again he would lick at the rum-and-Coke mixture between my knees.

Pop is a dummy. A native of Foschini in Zeerust. My companion on many solo trips.

We drove through Kimberley in the small hours and just past the Horseshoe Motel, under an acacia in the veld, I noticed a caravan. A light was on. *Fortune Teller*, proclaimed a red-and-white banner as I sped past.

Fortune teller? I had always wondered whether they are really able to. What does the future hold for anyone? My Dutch Reformed upbringing had made me conservative and dabbling in the future was not something to be trifled with.

I stepped on the brake and turned the loaded bakkie around, heading towards my future. Dog was asleep and Pop didn't say a word. The midnight hour was at hand.

In my own way I'm a "tinker" in the Irish sense of the word. I always want to know what's on the other side of a koppie. If there happens to be another one, I want to see what's on the other side of that. In this way a man can keep travelling to hell 'n gone. People like us are gypsies. Normal people don't always understand. Nowhere in Europe has the gypsy really been welcome. Landless travellers en route to nowhere.

I pulled up. I couldn't leave the sawn-off shotgun in the bakkie. Arrayed in bandana, dust coat, bracelets and earring, I

107

knocked at the door. Dirty and ugly – a terrifying sight at midnight.

A blonde girl opened the door.

"It's late," I said, "but my future is beckoning."

'Yes, it's late. I'll ask my mother."

"A hundred rand," she said on her return.

"It's a bargain," I replied and stepped in to face my future.

The little woman was in bed – the blanket pulled up to her chin. She wasn't very old, but suffering and life's hard lessons had left their mark on her face. After an exchange between mother and daughter in a strange language, the girl left the caravan. My guess was Polish or Rumanian.

I was shrewd enough not to give anything away. Just like me, occasionally playing the role of sangoma for urban blacks, the seer into the future bases his or her findings on the other person's words and actions.

I introduced myself and put down the shotgun. She drew the blanket higher up as I sat down at the foot of her bed.

"Tell me about myself."

"You drink a lot."

Logical – my breath smelt of rum, my eyes were bleary and my left cheek showed a tinge of Hemingway.

"You're a fortune teller too."

Oops. Touché.

And right there I realised that there was bugger all I wanted to know about my future, because that would just be spoiling the fun. So I told her her own story: Of not belonging. Of suffering. Of being an outcast. Of Poland. Of being under a tree outside Kimberley. Of predicting the future to an apparition like me after midnight.

She drew up her blanket even higher.

When I got up to leave, she gave me back my hundred rand. I rolled it up tightly, placed it in her worker's palm and kissed her on the head.

"Who are you?" she asked.

"Just a gypsy," I replied and left the caravan to return to my here and now, to Pop and Dog and my bakkie.

I had only done eleven kilometres in the dark when I realised I had left my bandana behind. I turned and drove back.

There was no caravan under the acacia. There was nothing, except my bandana, draped over a jakkalspisbossie.

Our land

The afternoon sun was fierce. We moved into the shade of a sweet thorn and drank thirstily from our water bottles. The smell of crushed red grass and dust hung heavily in the air. I wiped the sweat from my eyes and saw the bloody scratches of swarthaak and sickle bush on my upper arm. I was thoroughly fed up and gave my twelve-year-old son, Marc, a worried look. His shoulders were slumped and the 308 looked like a tree trunk in the little fellow's hands.

"Are you managing?"

"Yes, Pa," he lied. It was his first hunting trip. We had been walking for two days without getting a proper shot at anything. I imagined it had stopped being fun for him a long time ago – he was just doing it for his dad now.

"Let's rest for a while, then we'll go back to camp."

"OK, Pa."

Suddenly, barely sixty metres ahead, the impala ram came sauntering through the mopane bush . . .

The camp fire blazed. On the coals the impala's heart, kidneys and lungs were sizzling. The young Nimrod's face still bore the bloody fingermarks, and his eyes were shining after the hunt. I realised again how Africa is bred into us. We would pine without the open spaces of this continent and its Southern Cross. That was why I was part-owner of that piece of Bushveld – Terra Nostra, our land.

The place was our escape from the bustle of the city. On weekends we camped there, checked the fences, recorded new arrivals among the giraffe population, made firebreaks, hacked out alien plants and counted zebra and blue wildebeest. We felt privileged – we could never let go of this piece of paradise.

When they shot and killed Piet Smook and took his car, I drove out to Terra Nostra.

I did the same when they broke in at Uncle Joe's and hit him on the head.

We saw the zebra give birth. My children and I followed the new arrival for a day or two and found him before the jackal

111

had started to eat. We skinned him – he had been born without stomach and intestines. The perfect miniature hide was so uniqe, so remarkable, that I just had to have it tanned and dressed.

In Marabastad they stabbed Christina Branca and took all her possessions. They robbed my parents twice. They stole my bakkie. Nanna was pushed at an automatic teller machine, and they grabbed her money.

And Francois, my brother-in-law, took my sister and their two children and left – for Canada. I hear that it's bloody cold there and they can't see the Southern Cross. They came back only once. It was for the birth of their third, Christiaan . . .

A job opportunity in the Western Cape finally made me pull up my roots too, and I left Terra Nostra and came to plant sweet thorn, camel thorn, fever tree and paperbark at the foot of Paarl Mountain. And in my bar lay the little zebra hide – to remind me how I missed our land. It was all I had left of it.

The little man was six years old when they came back for a visit. My sister and her pale snow-children. I made hardekool fires and cooked large chunks of meat. We drank Cape white and dipped biltong in chutney. There were pumpkin fritters and bread pudding.

"Ma, Ma, a zebra skin!" the little boy exclaimed in Canadian Afrikaans and, like Racheltjie de Beer in front of the anthill in days of old, he threw himself down on the hide and lay there all evening.

Later that night: "Oom, how much does a zebra skin cost?"

"Man, if you have to buy it already dressed, I suppose between R10 000 and R13 000."

"Gosh!"

"If you shoot him yourself, the zebra is going to cost you about R2 500 and about another R5 000 to dress the skin. That way you'll save quite a bit of money."

"Oh."

And he lay down on Terra Nostra's little zebra.

112

It was late at night. By that time his mother and the rest of us had progressed to sweet wine.

"Oom, when we come back, will you take me to the veld so that I can shoot a zebra?" he pleaded.

If Africa is in your blood . . .

They left, down the coast, to celebrate Christmas with our parents. I am afraid of family Christmases and had been planning to skip this one too. In my bar lay my little zebra hide . . .

Early on the morning before Christmas I pushed the nose of the bakkie in the direction of the Eastern Cape.

My mother's Christmas tree twinkled joyfully in the beach cottage at Boknes. The snow-children twittered excitedly around the wrapped gifts.

"What are you doing here?" they asked.

Wordlessly I handed over my last piece of our land. And left. They should never have allowed him to be born here . . .

Sekkab Annan

"The flight from Tel Aviv was early. It landed two hours ago."

Surprised, I looked at the small Jewish lady in front of me, barely reaching up to my chest. For a moment I had forgotten that only my eyes are visible. What the hell would I want with the flight from Tel Aviv? I was waiting for the one from Brussels. I glanced up at the screen. It was flashing: *Tel Aviv has landed* . . .

Ignoring the Jewish matron, I looked out over the crowd of undersized Portuguese gathered in the arrivals hall at Lissabon airport. The two of us towered head and shoulders above these short people. Suddenly I became aware of two sallow, hook-nosed men, neatly clad in suits, watching us from a distance. Warily they began to close in. What was happening here? One looked me in the eye and flipped open his jacket archly. Under his armpit was an immense revolver. I looked at Ferdi, who, completely oblivious, was feasting his eyes on the Portuguese girls.

"Ouboet, there's big shit here. Where can the flight from Brussels be?" I muttered from the corner of my mouth.

The man with the revolver stepped up to me and asked in a threatening tone: "Who are you? Is this a joke? What are you doing here?"

He fumbled under his jacket and I thought, son of a bitch, I'm going to get shot right here in the middle of a crowd of Portuguese, and I don't even know why. He pulled out a badge and pushed it under my nose. Through the slit in the fabric I read: *Mossad.*

Suddenly the penny dropped . . .

The Dades gorge that ends in the Hammada, or the Moroccan pre-Sahara, is a remarkably beautiful place. Sheer cliffs rise hundreds of metres into the air. A babbling stream runs down to the Boumalne oasis. The picturesque mud dwellings of Ait Oudiner nestle against the cliffs as if they have been carved out of the rock face. Berbers herding sheep and goats deeper into the valley, passed below us.

We basked in the pleasant winter sun.

For the past two months or so Ferdi and I had been living at close quarters and often under appalling conditions. We had begun to get on each other's nerves and the smallest thing tended to become hugely irritating. We were sitting on the veranda of a small hotel. The Moroccan hotelier was preparing a Berber omelette. We were going to share it, for our funds were depleted.

While we were waiting for the omelette, I was making notes in my diary. Our travels had taken us through West Africa. From the Ivory Coast to Timbuktu in Mali, through Senegal and Mauritania and finally to Morocco. Public transport was precarious and the overnight accommodation on offer was no more than foul, cockroach-infested fifth-rate dumps.

Ferdi had nothing to occupy himself with and couldn't sit still. He began talking nonsense while I was trying to write. I ignored him. He got up, walked across the road and sat down on a rock. Before long he came back and resumed his senseless chatter. When I showed no reaction, he asked: "Do you hear what I'm saying?" I was beginning to get pissed off. To add fuel to the fire, he began to hum a tune: "Datte we toffe jongens zijn, dat wille we weten", or something to that effect. Incessantly.

The omelette was prepared on an open fire in a pottery container shaped like a shepherd's hat, and served up immediately. You remove the lid of the hat and tuck into the steaming contents. While we were telling each other how we had overindulged, the owner brought another bowl of potato chips. "Stuffed" as he pretended to be, Ferdi took the gap and devoured the chips like a crusher before I could even reach out my hand. Now I was thoroughly pissed off. I took a walk to escape from his presence, and from my own irritation.

On my return I rearranged the contents of my backpack yet again. We made our own supper, though there was not much food left. We didn't have much to say to each other and prepared the dried vegetables, two-minute noodles and tinned sardines in silence. Our trip together was coming to an end, for in a few days' time my wife would be joining us in Portugal. An idea came to us simultaneously. There and then we started planning her reception. We would dress up in desert garb and Ninja headdresses, hold up a sign with her name written backwards, followed by an Arab stop sign, and see whether she would recognise us.

We found it hilarious, imagining how she would search for a familiar face and at last, panic-stricken and desperate in a strange country, would ask two Arabs for help. The ice was broken between us and the irritation immediately forgotten.

. . . because here were two enormous Palestinian terrorists, towering head and shoulders above every other person. And the Tel Aviv flight had just landed.

A sidelong glance at the flashing screen told me that the connecting flight from Brussels with my darling wife on board had also landed. It seemed likely that there would be no welcoming committee for her after all – Boer or Arab.

I tried to explain the situation to the members of the Israeli secret service. I was struggling to make myself clearly heard through the layers of fabric and I could see they didn't believe me. They took up their positions beside Ferdi and me, their hands inside their jackets.

Then Nanna came walking down the ramp. She scanned the sea of faces, put on a shitty little smile, made a beeline for us and said, "Are you crazy, or what? Everyone can see you're not Arabs."

The plan

I noticed her beauty as he brought her to the table in the secluded restaurant. Stylishly dressed, with a black Diane Keaton hat perched diagonally on her head. I've always had a thing about a hat.

"Thank you for meeting us here." He put out his hand. "The less we are seen together, the better for everyone concerned."

I knew him well; he was my friend. I did not know the girl – she was a surprise to me. I did know his wife.

My greatest pleasure is making people happy. I am happiest amid the beauty of nature; that's why I like taking people into the wild in the hope that they will be able to take the same inspiration home with them. Unfortunately nature can take its toll, especially in the areas where I venture. It remains my responsibility to bring everyone back alive. With large groups I sometimes need a support crew. These are men experienced in emergencies, who can assess a situation and act without delay. My friend was one of those. I trusted him with my own life and the lives of others.

I was amazed by her beauty. She was porcelain pale, with blonde hair that framed her face under the brim of the hat.

"We want to ask you a favour," he said. I gave him a questioning look. "I want her to go with us."

I summed up the situation – the background was unknown to me but the repercussions were obvious.

"Hell, Ouboet, a lot of your friends will be going along. What will they say?"

"I don't give a damn!"

I looked at her. The large blue eyes were misty and the manicured hands were clasped together.

I wanted to protect him. "Do you know what you're doing?"

"She was my first love, but we never . . . finished it properly – the twists and turns of life made us pursue our own paths. Now, twenty years later, she's come to tell me that she's dying. We don't want to leave things unfinished . . ."

The fragile appearance of the girl in front of me suddenly made sense.

"She has never been where we're going. Let's call it a last wish," he played on my feelings.

"Bliksem, Ouboet, even healthy people die out there."

"I'll look after her."

"I need you to look after the others," I snapped. "What are the medical implications – can she walk, can she carry a backpack? What about her heart, her mind? You know, people have been known to die. I can't afford that."

For the first time she spoke in a soft voice. "I promise not to die until we've finished."

And right there I chucked all logic overboard. Who was I to begrudge someone their last wish? So we began to plan her first and last hike through the desert. I ended with, "There are two conditions, though – I'm going to watch her during the three-day trip up and I'll make my final decision before we go in. And there's no way you're going to drop me and not go on the hike. I need you as back-up."

They arrived at the departure point separately, as "strangers", but once we were on our way and people began to relax, they moved towards each other quite openly. She laughed and was clearly enjoying herself, and I was delighted. Our other friends began to make snide remarks behind his back: "Seems like he's a man with a plan." I just smiled. The fact that she was seizing the day was enough for me. It was good.

It was the night before we were to go in. The contents of backpacks were being rearranged and last minute organisation completed.

"Ouboet, things are looking good – I think there's a great adventure ahead," I said.

"We're not going along – we'll be waiting for you at the exit," he answered.

I was instantly furious. Had this been his plan all along and had I just been a pawn in his game?

"You're forgetting our agreement," I snapped.

"She's very ill and I'm not leaving her on her own!"

She died two months later. During that time they never saw each other again. But I think they finished it – the hike was not the important thing, after all.

On the wings of Bonnies

I'm usually the one on the road – this time it was my dear wife, however, and I was stuck with the household and kids. In between cooking, carting kids around, school work, looking after dogs, ironing, and washing dishes, I was also trying to get to the office. I consoled myself with the temporary nature of the situation and when the pressure became too much, I poured some Bonnies.

My friend Kalie introduced me to this particular brand of liquid refreshment. It was a year or two previously, when I had arrived in Paarl from the Transvaal, with bag and baggage. Pulling up my roots was difficult for me, as was adjusting. The Bonnies helped me to find the mountains more beautiful day by day.

"Pa, we need wings," my daughter said.

"What for?" I asked and imagined her soaring from Paarl Rock, down to the Main Street. She explained: She'd been elected cheerleader for her school and the theme for their athletics meeting was *Lord of the Rings*, fairies and all. As she explained, I realised we weren't talking Sunday School wings here, but humungous cherubic pinions.

"What about the other mothers?" I tried to get out of it.

"The other cheerleaders are boarders. Their mothers are on farms somewhere in the Karoo," she shattered my final hope.

"We must have four sets by Monday," she said. It was twelve noon on Saturday.

I hurried to the fabric shop for chiffon and silk. Then to the hardware store for galvanised and binding wire. During the first attempt I realised bending wire into shape wasn't my forte, and not even propellers and turbines would get those wings into the air. The distress and disappointment in my child's eyes made my heart sink into my boots. Her father, who had taken her to the top of Kilimanjaro, couldn't even produce a set of wings.

Over a glass of Bonnies I suddenly remembered Prince, the wire car king of Franschhoek. And we sped off to Franschhoek – no, the man is in Paarl these days, we were told, so we sped back.

"Sure," he said, "it's easy. I'll deliver them by tomorrow afternoon."

The battle has been won, I thought thankfully.

On Sunday afternoon I tried to bring fabric and wire together and realised: Bonnies was going to be absolutely no help to me here.

With a hurried prayer I answered the doorbell and, sure enough, in front of me stood Reverend Elsje, my spiritual leader from up north. A surprise visit? Coincidence . . .?

"Dominee, there's no time for prayers today – I need wings," I blurted out without a greeting.

"Brother, you'll only get them up there . . ."

I explained, cracked a bottle of Bonnies and poured. The Reverend gave the wire and chiffon one look and said: "Brother, there's no way we're going to sew this fabric to this wire, we'll have to glue."

And that night the Reverend burned her fingers with the glue gun as she glued those wings together one by one. And I kept pouring Bonnies.

By the early hours I was furnished with four sets of wings, and while she was cooling her fingers in the ice bucket and taking a sip, the Reverend declared: "Brother, you'll probably arrive up there before me, especially with these wings and all . . . Please just tell them I don't want a job in the wing factory, but they might want to consider me for the water-in-wine department."

She did her bit, after all, so I'll do mine.

A view of Everest

I received a letter today:

Hi, how are you? I am fine here. I hope you are well in there. Please convey my "namaste" to all our four friends. I found you all very well people. I did many enjoy with you.

Yours sincerely

Lakpa Sherpa

And suddenly I was back in Nepal. The land with the highest mountains in the world. The land with a religious diversity that makes you stop and think. A land with incredibly friendly people. Dirt poor, but with hearts as big as the grace of God.

We were four friends with time on our hands and some loose cash available, who decided to explore the land where Mongol and Indo-European finally met. With backpacks, we planned to venture into the wilderness – crossing mountains which our continent, Africa, can only wonder about. Foremost, however, was that we were not interested in the usual routes. We wanted to go to places where we were unlikely to meet another Westerner.

After a lengthy flight we invaded Katmandu airport like typical tourists. In spite of our bravado, we were scared shitless of what lay ahead. This wasn't our part of the world! Our reception in the strange land was warm and open-hearted. A luxurious hotel, by African standards, awaited us. Guided tours to Patan and Bhaktapur – their temples and culture – merely emphasised how surreal it was being there.

But the mountains were our true destination. High up in the mountains, the small plane arrived rather than landed. The pilot virtually collided with the short runway, surrounded by massive peaks. Shakily we got out, and Lakpa Sherpa welcomed us with "namaste". For the next ten days he would be our guide, interpreter and friend. With only one eye – he had lost the other in an avalanche on the slopes of the Gyachung Kang mountain – he led us into a wasteland of snow, glaciers and ice.

Though the country is rich in heart-stopping scenic beauty and the people enjoy a wonderful quality of life, the average Nepalese is poor. Jobs are scarce. A one-eyed ex-high-altitude

126

mountaineering Sherpa lives on borrowed time and every cent earned was accepted gratefully and immediately handed over to his people in the Khumbu valley. Their needs were simple, and staple food consisted of dal bhat – rice and a dipping sauce concocted from vegetables.

During the time we spent with Lakpa and his team we witnessed perseverance and endurance for the sake of economic survival that no Westerner can fully comprehend. Fathers and sons facing snowstorms in bare feet, with sixty-kilogram packs on their backs, while we were huddled together, wondering whether we would survive to see the next day. We encountered poverty, but also unbelievable goodwill towards others. People with less than nothing took us, prosperous Westerners, into their homes and offered us their last morsel of food.

On our return we found ourselves back in Katmandu, the capital city. It was a riot of colours, sounds and smells. With the little money we had, we were able to buy a lot for the people at home. Pashminas were acquired for next to nothing and large quantities of beer guzzled. We were "rich", and Nepal was on the receiving end.

A free day saw us book a flight across Everest. At R600 for a one-hour flight, it was costly even for us. We set out for the plane. The four of us and a group of French organisers of the Raid Gauloises, an international endurance competition. They were all clad in African khaki. It was clear that the company was paying for their excursion. Last to board the sixteen-seater plane was a shy Nepalese girl. She found a seat diagonally in front of me. I had the lookout window on my side – at that price, at least you had to be able to see, I thought.

She was neatly turned out and had a small camera – just a little snap-shitter – that she was clutching in her hand. When she sat down, I saw the anticipation in her brown eyes. How much and for how long had she saved up for this experience?

As the plane taxied to the runway, I saw she was battling to buckle up and I realised it was probably her first time in a plane.

Realising that my appearance usually makes women run away and babies cry, I leaned across carefully – before she could recoil with fright – and fastened her seatbelt. Her "dhanyabad" – thank you – was soft and timid.

The anticipation and excitement in her eyes made me feel guilty. Here I was, a tourist with money. And she, a native of this country, probably had to use her life savings just to be able to say: "I saw the highest my country and the world have to offer."

The plane gained altitude and I kept watching her. During takeoff she was tense but she soon began to look around, taking a photo of the cockpit at the front. The French at the back were rowdy.

And then, on the left, the Himalayas came into view. It was an incredible sight, this wilderness of glaciers and rugged mountains. It was scary. I identified two peaks, Numbur and Karyolung. A few days before, we had camped at the glaciers and frozen lakes at the foot of those mountains. I became aware of soft breathing and realised the Nepalese girl was trying to see through the window, which I was blocking completely. The French were crowding around the other windows.

She tried to stop me as I got up to give her my window seat. No, dammit, I thought, I may still return one day – she would not. Of the rest I didn't see much. I stared instead at her profile outlined against the icy slopes of the Himalayas. It was enough for me to witness the joy and ecstacy this person was experiencing. I was told we had flown over Everest too – I hadn't seen it, but that was OK.

When it was over, she asked someone to take a photograph of the two of us. I laughed and imagined she would tell people that she had even come across a yeti.

Before we landed, she told me she was a teacher, whose subject was Nepalese history. In her country teachers were allowed to fly for free – she could return the next day, if she so wished.

Mignon's forest

At the top end of Enslin Street, on the slopes of Paarl Mountain, there used to be a pine forest. Majestic, gnarled pine trees. For more than two centuries they had kept their swaying vigil over Paarl Valley.

My aging body had forced me to start training before every proposed hiking trip or expedition. But there is nothing I detest more than putting on my running shoes and racing up and down the streets, gasping for breath. Even worse is sprinting in one place, claustrophobically stuffy, somewhere in a gymnasium. Not to mention weaving through cars on a bicycle, dressed in a bright clown suit. If I have to train, I prefer to put my boots on, throw a few bricks in my backpack and head for the nearest piece of veld.

Doringkloof in Pretoria was difficult. There was a three-kilometre walk on a tarred road before I could jump over the fence to get into the Irene koppies. Through hip-high Highveld grass, up the hill, I tried to hammer my old body into shape again. Paarl is different: out through the front door, up Enslin Street's steep incline, through the forest, and up to Paarl Rock.

The pine forest was where I paused for the first time to breathe. Not necessarily because I was tired, but because of the scenery. Footpaths took you higher and higher up the mountain. At the overhanging rock a family of dwarfs might call out a friendly greeting, while fairies might dance joyfully ahead of you at the bend, just before you reached the Jan Phillips Drive. Early in the morning, if you were lucky, you might see the elves playing skittles on the moss at the reservoir. Gone was all fatigue as you emerged into the fynbos. Then you pushed your body and you *could*, because you knew when you returned, the cool, mysterious world of Mignon's forest would be waiting.

Mignon . . . inevitably such a beautiful place had to have a princess, and it was while I was training for a proposed marathon hike somewhere in the deserts of Namibia that I paused for breath, panting, head hanging, somewhere at the edge of the forest.

"I see you walking in the forest regularly – isn't it beautiful here?" I heard a voice say. I gazed at her in wonder. Bright red hair, greyish green eyes – the silver rings on the manicured hands drew my attention. Neatly clad in a flowing garment of earthy chiffon.

"You know, people have come to tell me they're going to chop down the forest."

And so I met Mignon. Mignon with the flaming hair and the forest in her eyes. A lad from the Boland had fetched her from the Transvaal as a young girl and built her a house thirty years ago. Here, where Paarl Mountain breathes. Perhaps to exorcise the separation from her people, her escape was into the forest. The forest became her and she became the forest.

"Over my dead body . . ." her soft voice rang in my ears as I forced myself, sweating, higher and higher up.

She came to report regularly, as I took a breather on my way up the mountain. She told me about her own as well as the forest's struggle for survival. About all the letters she had written to the municipality. About the people of the Heritage Trust whom she had implored to help, about pleading with one organisation and appealing to another. And as the weeks passed, the dejection and helplessness began to show in her eyes. I lowered my head and climbed through Mignon's forest, higher and higher.

The day before my departure for the desert the trucks, cranes and power saws gathered at the top end of Enslin Street. I turned away, packed my rucksack and left.

They told me afterwards that Paarl Mountain had burned that night.

And when the flames had reached the pine trees, Mignon with the flaming red hair had walked into the forest.

131

Der Reiter von Eros

"How do you feel about walking 780 km through the desert?" Frik asked. It was a stupid question and he knew it. To hike with backpack and boots is one of my greatest delights . . . and into the desert – where my heart grows small again.

Deserts have always fascinated me. Where the stars are at their brightest, and the setting sun forces you to pause. Where the piercing night chill secretly makes you long for tomorrow's blistering heat. It's the sweltering daytime, however, that holds the possibility of death, for in the desert you die. It's where the word "respect" gets new meaning, for you don't play with the desert – it will fuck you up, for sure.

"When are we leaving?" was the anticipated reply, and so I became part of an expedition to raise funds for the Rhino and Elephant Foundation, and specifically for the desert elephant and Damara rhinoceros, which were being hunted relentlessly by poachers.

Southern Africa is desert per definition. It is an arid country. The Karoo, Bushmanland, the Kalahari and the Namib. Each of these regions has its own enchantment. The ostensible nothingness, the koppie-sheep-bush Karoo, the red-dune-camel-thorn-green Kalahari, the salt-pan-waving-grass-open Bushmanland, and then the apparently lifeless gravel surfaces and shifting dunes of the Namib.

The hike was planned. From Opuwa in Northern Kaokoland to Kaoko Otavi, through Robbie's Pass to Sesfontein. Wêreldsend via Palmwag, then Twyfelfontein, past the Brandberg, down along the Ugab to the Messum Crater. Through the White Namib, turning right at the Omaruru River and then to the sea at Wlotskas Baken, until we reached Swakop.

A hell of a distance.

My dad first told me about deserts. I was young. The story of Heinrich Bart and René Caillé through the Sahara, of Marco Polo through the Gobi. The wreck of the *Dunedin Star* along the Skeleton Coast. Stories of survival. I realised even then that the desert is no man's friend. I remember the story about "der Reiter von Eros" – an illusory figure, clad in the uniform of the old German Schutztruppen, who warned hunters, adventurers and random passers-by against imminent danger.

The most important thing on a hike through the desert is water. You need at least three to four litres per day, excluding what is needed to wash. A litre of water weighs a kilogram – we were going to walk 32 km per day, so it would be physically impossible to carry more than a three-day supply. We planned carefully. There would be microlight aircraft throwing down water; Himbas and Damaras who knew of fountains and wells; a support team that would rendezvous with us if the terrain allowed it. In addition, there was always hope . . . hope of an unexpected dampness.

And we walked. It became the adventure of a lifetime. It was up at first light, pack the rucksack and blunder on. The terrain varied between gravel plains and sand, and basalt rocks that chewed at your ankles. For days on end not even a patch of shade. At noon you covered your head with your rucksack to escape the worst of the sun. We walked on moonlit nights to protect ourselves against the fury of the day. But at the end of every day we came "home". When the sun set, we pitched camp – a camp that became home. Groundsheet became hallway carpet. A tuft of grass in an enamel mug became a flower arrangement for the sitting room and a pile of sand or a rock served as a sofa. A blazing fire or gas stove marked out our inner circle. And comrades became family. We spoke about today and speculated about tomorrow, and tomorrow we would pick up our rucksacks once again.

April 18: Today we reached the dry bed of the Ugab. Must say, our water is running low. I walk with a pebble permanently under the tongue not to drink – don't know whether we'll meet up with the support crew day after tomorrow. Actually everyone is still strong. We've been at it for three weeks today. Frik, the oldest, might look older, but he's strong as an ox. Patzer strides comfortably with the heavy camera bag, swinging those hips like a camel. Now and then a feeble, shitty joke. Grant's feet are ru-

ined, but he remains in the lead, the compass at times spinning uncontrollably among the ironstone formations.

I could swear I heard thunder . . .

What makes this desert world of ours even more remarkable is the realisation that there used to be water here. Centuries ago dinosaurs gambolled in the lakes of the Kalahari. The Okavango is still trying to find its way back to the sea. In the meantime it deltas into the sand. Dry riverbeds or omurambas are chiselled evidence of furious waters that have tried to tame the desert.

Grant: "Let's call it a day. According to the map we've done 33 km. Tonight there's a three-quarter moon. Perhaps we can rest tomorrow and walk in the evening."

Under an ana tree that had taken root obstinately in the dry riverbed we threw down our backpacks. The river had carved a deep ravine here and we would be able to settle in, sheltered from the piercing desert wind.

Driftwood was gathered and we made ourselves a home. The fire burned high as we lay bundled in our sleeping bags, talking shit. The wind whirled across the river bank, throwing up dust. Coffee simmered on the side. It was good.

I realised it was going to be a cold evening and luckily we were out of the wind. I buried some coals in the sand and placed my sleeping bag on top.

"Guten abend, Herren." I looked up, startled. In the circle of the firelight stood a man, clad in the uniform of the former German Schutztruppen. He was holding a horse by its reins. We were taken aback – another human being in these parts, tonight?

"Wie geht's?" We stared, open-mouthed.

"Gut danke und dir? Willkommen. Kaffee? Setze dich," my matric German came gushing out.

And he threw the reins over an ana branch and came to stand next to the fire.

Flustered, Patzer poured coffee.

"Danke, meine Herren. Dieser Platz ist eine gefährliche Lage. Es ist besser am Ufer."

Two sips and he put the mug down, mounted his horse and rode into the dark.

We looked at one another.

"What the fuck did he say?" asked Frik.

"We mustn't sleep in the riverbed – it's dangerous," I said.

"Balls, man, its bloody cold up there and we're all settled in," Grant flared up.

We left it there, but conversation was subdued and we turned towards dreamland.

It was two o'clock in the morning when I woke. I felt uneasy. Something was bothering me. I woke everyone else.

"Boys, I'm going to sleep on the river bank." I gathered my stuff together. I saw Frik and Patzer collecting their things too. Grant refused to budge.

It was bloody cold at the top and the wind was unpleasant. We tried to get comfortable. Tomorrow would be a long day.

"Grant," I said urgently. "Don't be like that. Come and join us up here." The hair on my neck stood on end.

And just as Grant was putting down his backpack next to ours, we became aware of an eerie rumbling. In the moonlight I saw a wall of water, with foam, rocks and tree trunks, roaring down the dry Ugab underneath us.

Gert Geloof

"Do you know Gert Geloof?"

And there she stood. Our glasses of pampelmoes stopped on their way to our mouths. We stood open-mouthed, staring at the desert nymph who had just been blown in through the door. Her suntanned face, accentuated by the pale ash blonde hair that hung to her shoulders, was grim and emotionless . . .

"Hoch das Bein, der Kaiser braucht Soldaten." Tossing down our drinks, we completed the toast in the bar at Helmeringhausen. Damn, she's pretty, I thought, studying the tanned legs that seemed to go on for ever, finally disappearing into the rolled-up khaki shorts.

There were nine of us, en route to Naukluft, where we were planning to hike in the barren desert mountains for eight days. These were hard men, but I saw the yearning on the faces of Kokkie and Dok. Paul said "Augh", and Kalie smiled lopsidedly.

She stood with her feet planted wide, staring at the occupants of the bar defiantly. "One day the Lord said to Gert, 'It's a sin to watch television,' so he chucked the TV through the window."

For a moment we were baffled, and even Carlos, who was never at a loss for words, was speechless.

"It was while he was sitting in church at Stampriet that the Lord spoke to him for the second time, saying, 'Gert, the drought is pinching, you must stop farming and start making money.' So he left everything and rented out his farm. A command answered in good faith."

It was as if a great weariness came over her. The lovely child had lost the spiritedness of a moment before. "I haven't seen my father for six years. If you meet up with him, tell him I miss him."

She turned around and left as abruptly as she had come.

We poured more pampelmoeses and chased down the sweetness with a Tafel beer, still dumbfounded by the sudden arrival and departure of the girl. Our spirits had been dampened too and, with the prospect of 200 kilometres of dirt road ahead, we took our leave.

A Namibian dirt road is a thing of beauty, but you have to know your stuff, because loose sand and gravel can make the rear end of a car behave very erratically. The soberest among us got behind the wheels. The road undulated straight ahead. It was like riding a roller coaster. Every height was blind and with your stomach in your knees you fervently hoped that the invisible stretch of road on the other side would lead straight down.

At the turn-off to the Zaris pass we came across the crumpled vehicles. It had been a head-on collision. We reached the Volla first. She lay slumped forward. The blonde hair . . . The lovely face lifeless and cut to ribbons. I hurried past. There was still life in the old Ford bakkie.

"Oom, Oom, are you all right?" The weather-beaten old man tried to focus.

"Oom, what's your name?"

"Gert," he muttered.

Half-man

Every once in a while a man needs to run away. To sneak away in the middle of the night without anyone knowing, realising full well that it could change everything. It might cost you your job; without a doubt your family will be packing your stuff into Checkers shopping bags – the only question is whether they're going to put your belongings in the garden shed or leave it outside in the rain.

These are the times when boundaries are shifted a bit and you know you'd better turn round before it's too late. But when the bakkie has passed Kuruman, you realise you're past the point of no return. If some day you should wish to go back, you'd just have to suffer the consequences. Running away doesn't always have to be for a reason – it can be a sudden impulse. It usually has no purpose either. It's a journey without a fixed plan or destination.

My flights are usually into the desert. Bushmanland, the Kalahari, the Namib and the Richtersveld. Where it can get so lonely that you get fed up with yourself. But the therapeutic value of steering the nose of the bakkie into the open road with the rousing Mantovani version of "Villa Rides" full-blast in your ears and a beer between your knees is unequalled. Going nowhere. Such journeys make me realise I am a man who wants to be a part of things, while at the same trying to keep to myself. That is why after a few days in the desert I'm likely to sit in the bar at Springbok for three consecutive days, listening to people argue about where the true borders of Bushmanland lie, and whether Pofadder really *is* the capital of these parts.

Cruising into Bushmanland, I was intrigued by the name of a saltpan on the map – Bosluispan. The gravel road stretched before me and I put my foot down to the tune of Bach's "Toccata and Fugue".

At Gamoep I turned left to Lekkerdrink.

Bushmanland is devoid of water. What little water there is, is so brackish that the meat of a freshly slaughtered sheep is instanty pickled. It's a grateful land, however, and a mere drop of

141

water makes the bushman grass grow tall. In the 1920s it was crown land and the stock farmers trekked around in search of water and pasture.

There were no fences. Natural migration of game was unrestricted and there was room for everyone.

The demarcation of farms changed the situation irreversibly. Boundary fences and wells that dried up have been the demise of many a farmer. Only empty ruins have remained, with names like Frummelbakkies, Tauseep, Onderste and Boonste Koos se Vlei, Kyngrypsbult and Riembreek.

At the farm Kleinputs I found a gate and came across the first person I had met all day.

"Good day, Oom. I'm looking for the way to Bosluispan, Oom," I said.

The man stared at me in amazement. Where did this Biblical figure spring from . . . and calling me "Oom" as well, he was probably thinking.

"Neef, it's just on the other side of this dune, about three kilometres to the west, but keep the gates closed and don't drive across the pan, or I'll have to come and pull you out with the tractor." He shook his head. "What are you doing here anyway? Not even *normal* people come here."

"Oom, it's the name Bosluis – I just want to see."

"Do you know about the graves beside the pan?" And it was right there that I stopped running away and began to follow the spoor of the Bosluisbasters.

Two centuries ago these parts harboured many people from different ethnic groups. Bushmen and Hottentots, Oorlams and Griquas, Jonker Afrikaner's people and Trekboers – and also the Basters. The Basters, proud of their name, were the result of brief liaisons between European men and Hottentot women. They were outcasts in the eyes of certain white communities, but considered themselves a cut above their Hottentot ancestors. They set great store on their own identity, though they also aspired to be accepted as equals by the white community. That was why marrying "upward", in other words finding a light-skinned partner, was desirable. Cattle and landownership were top priority. A group from Worcester settled in the Vanrhynsdorp district and began to accrue their own livestock as bywoners and foremen. Some obtained land and married into the white community.

From the crest of the dune I looked out across the pan below. It was the Makgadikgadi in smaller format. I estimated it at about seven kilometres long and three kilometres wide. It was impressive, this snow-white salt pan among red dunes and bushman grass. Etched against the western horizon were a lone tree and the remains of ramshackle buildings.

I left the sandy track in four-wheel mode. The ruins gave nothing away. Among the bushes lay a few graves – mostly of children. Meyer, Cloete, Groenewald, Basson and Volmoer, I read.

Can one truly make a living in this barren thirstland?

The solitude was oppressive.

When General Manie Maritz invaded the Cape with his Boer commando, it was his goal to quell all possible support for the British. The majority of the white population of Bushmanland was well disposed towards the Boers – a question mark hung over the rest.

Sjambok and violent actions were Manie's way of enforcing loyalty. His aides crushed the skulls of two inhabitants of Leliesfontein against the walls of the mission church after they had attacked the general (possibly in self-defence). Today, a century later, the blood stains are still visible through the layers of whitewash when the walls get wet.

At Vanrhynsdorp he laid into the Basters with the sjambok and they were literally chased into the desert. The dispersed population regrouped at Bosluis. The stock farmers trekked away in search of pasture, but returned to Bosluis regularly for church services. The rest scraped salt, which transport riders sold for them in Upington and Port Nolloth.

I sat on a rock, looking out over the pan and the rolling red dunes. What had become of the displaced people who had tried

143

to eke out an existence here? I was filled with sadness and fury at the people and ethnic groups who had lost their language, land and culture.

Where are the Bushmen, the Griquas and the Namas today?

Where are the Bosluis basters?

The road took me to Klawermuis, then Brabees and Diksand, and on to Suurwater. I gave Springbok a wide berth – I wasn't looking for company just yet.

It was sweltering as I drove into Eksteensfontein in the Richtersveld. The wind blew the limy sand into nostril and eye. I had been away from home for a long time and my family had no idea what had become of me. For all I knew, someone had already replaced me in society. I felt as if I did not belong anywhere any more. I was tired of running away, but I wanted to take one last photograph of the halfmens – the half-man – a hardy aloe-like plant that grows and flourishes in those parts. This strange man-sized cactus grows only against the northern slopes of the rocky mountains in that area, and then only in specific spots.

The sun glittered blindingly on the white earth and the hot wind gusted, while dust devils pitched and swirled tumbleweeds between the white buildings. Not a soul was out in the streets. This was a remorseless region.

My throat was craving a beer. A faded Castle sign flapped in the wind, proclaiming *Cold beer and ice.*

Gratefully I shut the door behind me. It was actually a cuca shop with two melamine tables for those who might need a rest. A weather-beaten Nama with a bottle of vaaljapie in front of him was occupying one of them. I sat down at the other with two cold beers.

I leaned across. "Meneer, where can I see the half-man around here?"

The vagueness did not leave his eyes. "First you must get a permit from Dirkie Volmoers. Then you follow the Stinkfontein River for about fifteen kilometres. There are a few on the northern slopes of the Rooiberg.

I introduced myself.

"Basson." He put out a wrinkled hand.

I remembered a little grave somewhere in Bushmanland.

"Basson? Where from, meneer?"

"The locals call us 'kommers' – 'comers' – from Bosluis. When the farmers began to erect fences, we couldn't make a living any more and we were forced to move here, to the reserve."

"But meneer, how does a man *stand* it here?

"No, meneer, it's only a half-man that can stand it here," he said and swallowed the last of his bottle.

Purgatory

And suddenly, unexpectedly, I was jerked to a standstill, for in front of me was a yawning abyss. Panic and the sudden disappearance of the riverbed made me drop to my knees as if in prayer. I was looking into a primeval world.

The scene that unfolded in front of me took my breath away. The unbelievably rugged cliffs and the rock pools below – could anyone be so privileged, so unexpectedly and in so unsolicited a way? I lifted my eyes in thanks.

It wasn't the first time I had had such a humbling experience. That moment when Creation lets you know – He is greater than you.

A waterfall on the Transkei Wild Coast plunging directly into the sea, with me underneath it, the waves of the wide ocean surging around me. The noise of the water and my skin drenched with sweetness and salt. Shouting, I gave thanks for the experience.

Years ago I ploughed through to the Orange River at Pella early one morning. There was no proper road – only a dot on the 1 to 50 000 map. I struggled on to Klein Pella – about 14 kilometres further.

As usual, the bakkie was loaded. The idea was to bushwhack along the banks of the Orange River on my own, from Klein Pella to Noordoewer via Goodhouse. There were cool boxes filled with beer, a bed roll and extra fuel jerry-canned onto the roof. There was also a 5-litre oil can tied in a bundle with a grill, cast-iron pot, chair and table . . .

Another special moment was a sunset in the Messum crater near the Brandberg in Namibia. Bedding placed under an overhanging rock with a view over the crater. Below, the ancient leaves of the old welwitschias snaking along the sand, waiting with cupped hands for the early-morning sea mist. Drink in hand, I lit my pipe. Then the sun tore itself to shreds in the barren wilderness, and I forgot to swallow. This time I said thanks in silence. And I wondered what I had done to deserve this beauty . . .

The faint trail took me deeper into the wasteland. At one

stage, as I was manoeuvring the bakkie through a gully in the rock, I realised I had passed the point of no return. At a Nama shepherd's matjieshuis I pulled over.

"Is this the way to Klein Pella, meneer?" I asked.

"Yes, Meester, but this isn't a road. Now and again we walk there with the donkeys."

If they can, so can I, I thought and took the bit between my teeth. But the further I progressed, the more I realised I was in deep shit. The terrain was becoming impassable. The riverbed in which I found myself plunged downward and boulder and rock made driving a harrowing experience.

I walked out on the Serengeti. As far as the eye could see – kilometre after kilometre – I was surrounded by wildebeest. "The gathering," the Masai had told me. Fuck the migration, I thought, and sent up another thank you. I was in heaven yet again!

It couldn't be that simple. What had I done? I wondered briefly.

I was pouring with sweat as I battled with the steering wheel. And in the noon sun a yawning chasm lay waiting. I had to go down there. I engaged the lowest gear of the 4x4, sent up a prayer and used the bakkie's compression to move down the slope.

Then the sun fell on the pebbles in the ravine below and the reflection was blinding, like a blazing fire. It was as if I had been struck by blindness, and, unable to see, I forged ahead. I was driving through hell. Stones scattered in every direction as the tyres battled to find a grip. I couldn't see a thing, but I heard the oil can fall. I was fighting for survival – I felt the bakkie list. There was hardly time to think, my sweaty hands were clenched around the steering wheel and I thought, oh fuck, I'm going to lose the bakkie. But then the engine droned on. At last I reached the opposite bank – and put my foot down. My table was smashed on a rock, but I wasn't about to stop. To stop would mean the end of the road. And all around me were fiery quartz and stones. Then I was through. Trembling, I poured a Namaqua gin and raised a glass to my escape from the inferno.

Yesterday I read in an old document: *Vagevuurskloof: Region some 6 km west of Pella, south of Pella se Berg. Afrikaans for 'purgatory ravine', the name was given by the 18th century traveller Colonel RJ Gordon in 1779 because it is strewn with quartz stones which give off sparks at the slightest touch and because Gordon's party traversed it with great difficulty.*

And then I understood the Catholic principle – you have to have been in hell before you can experience heaven.

A moer of a party at an empty graveside

"While Ouma Magrieta was trying to scratch the Statebijbel out of the fire with a yoke, the Khakis fired through the windows into the house and Catharina Maria Uys, twelve years old, dropped the crockery she had been trying to save. And as she fell, she crawled out of the burning farmhouse at Palmietfontein near Heilbron."

I saw my father swallow hard. He was a soldier and did not cry easily.

"They fled in front of the English and escaped being taken to a concentration camp. Oupa Uys fell at Nicholson's Neck and Ouma returned to a farm that was wasted and empty."

Now my father was struggling.

"Maria Uys, my mother and your grandmother, saw a century pass. Probably one of the most interesting centuries. She lived through two World Wars, the advent of the motorcar, moon landings, depression years, atom bombs, heart transplants . . ."

My grandmother's descendants were sitting in the church at Harmoniehof, listening to her youngest having the last official say.

"Her husband, my father, died when I was three months old," my father continued. "A champion for the Afrikaner and the Republican ideal. The widow Bakkes never got married again, but she continued to carve out a future for her three children and herself."

I felt very sorry for my father.

I cast a sidelong glance at my cousins and brothers. They were damned hard men: a mercenary in the Belgian Congo, a pilot in Botswana, a reckless traveller of no fixed address, merciless businessmen, adventurers . . . One had even been half-eaten by a crocodile. We seldom saw one another, but when there was trouble, we closed ranks.

The widow Bakkes. The matriarch.

Towards the end, aged eighty-five, she was difficult. The retirement home where we sometimes lunched on Sundays was her last stop. She had decided herself that the time had come . . .

With hair neatly coiled under a hairnet, the former matriarch and pack leader waited impatiently for the Lord to come and fetch her. It got so bad that she was always late for any appointment or excursion, to the exasperation of her progeny.

When my brother Marius came to fetch her for my wedding, she had not even put on her stockings yet. Instead, she was lying in bed, waiting for Jesus.

"Ma, you'll be late for your own funeral one day," my father had always chastised her good-naturedly.

My father was nearing the end of his speech. Heaven knows – if I have to speak like that about *him* one day, I won't make it, I thought.

The service in Pretoria was over. When my grandfather died sixty years before, Ouma had unfortunately secured a plot next to his in Braamfontein, Johannesburg. That was where we were now heading to bid Ouma farewell at her final resting place. As a funeral procession was impractical, we set off individually through the heavy traffic.

One by one we gathered at the graveside. The grave was lined with green. The cousins were standing around. Old stories were recalled. New adventures were shared. Here and there a shot or a bottle came to light.

And a moer of a party took place at the empty graveside, because the hearse had got lost and Ouma Bakkes was late for her own funeral.

Ambassador

It was hard to believe, but I was standing in the dusty streets of Timbuktu. Many people think it doesn't exist at all, or that it's just the name of some place to hell 'n gone at the back of beyond. They're right in one respect – the place *is* to hell 'n gone. But it does exist. In the middle of the Sahara, in Mali, West Africa.

Our journey started six and a half thousand kilometres to the south. We travelled to Abidjan on the Ivory Coast by air. From there we had planned to travel across West Africa to Europe, using public transport and hitching rides. It didn't bode well for two men who couldn't speak a word of French.

The moment we set foot in West Africa, we were inundated by swarms of taxi drivers, guides, curio sellers, beggars, swindlers and enquirers. Everyone chattered in French, and it was clear that they all wanted something from us – chiefly money. It was almost impossible to shake them off – not even plain bad manners or cursing in Afrikaans could do the trick. Wherever we went, this entourage made privacy and true enjoyment impossible.

We couldn't wait to leave Abidjan and its retinue behind. We set out by bus for Karogo in the north, where a new team of blue-arsed flies and hangers-on would be waiting to entertain us "for a consideration". The bus journey to Mopti on the Niger River was an adventure in itself. We noticed the bus only when our luggage was being loaded (at extra cost, of course). It was a Mercedes with large, dome-shaped windows, but from a distance it appeared twisted, like a koeksister. There was no roof carrier, but the furniture of seven households had already been tied to the roof with ropes passed through holes in the body. On closer inspection we saw the outer casings of the headlights were missing, and to protect the bulbs against the rain they had been covered with transparent bread bags. The perspex windscreen was cracked and someone had fixed it with galvanised wire. From the front the bus looked like Dr Frankenstein's monster. But if we had found the exterior of the bus suspect, the battered chaos inside was even worse.

The seats were in tatters, with stuffing protruding everywhere. The windows could not open and where the rear window should have been, there was a steel plate. The bus was literally in three pieces, held together with nuts and bolts. The roof was held up by three iron posts that were bolted to the floor. The vehicle was horrendously dirty and red dust clung to the bits of upholstery that were still intact.

It was pitch-dark and raining as the wreck departed on its 600-kilometre journey to Mopti. We tried to settle in comfortably, but diesel fumes, hay-fever-producing dust and swarming cockroaches made all efforts to relax impossible. Moreover, initial brief supplications soon developed into a marathon prayer session – fervent petitions that we might arrive at our destination in one piece. My friend had also surrendered to his fate. Where he was normally able to find something positive in any shitty situation, this time he could only recommend that we find seats on the left side of the bus. That way, should the driver contrive to kill himself, at least we would be sitting on the opposite side.

Nowadays Timbuktu, once a city with 100 000 inhabitants and universities and colleges, is a town with a population of approximately 15 000. It is slowly but surely being swallowed by the Sahara desert. The city dates back to 1100 AD, when a group of Touareg nomads settled there. In 1494 Leo Africanus, a well-travelled Spanish Moor, paid a visit to the city and commented on the large number of doctors, lawyers and theologians that he had encountered there. But by the time that the first European explorers arrived there in the nineteenth century, it was already in decline.

We looked around us. Where to now? All the streets consisted of sand and dust. All the mud buildings looked the same. All the people were swaddled in kaftans and cloths. We set out for the police station, because obtaining a stamp of approval from the police is a requirement in every town in Mali. The idea is that the entire town should be made aware of the strangers at their gates.

We suddenly realised that, for the first time in Africa, we were being left in peace. It was peculiar. Because the normal route across the Sahara through Algeria had fallen into disuse, owing to the Touareg uprisings in the country, strangers didn't call here any more. Surely anyone who did come was a potential source of income?

We hoped that a cold beer would be available somewhere. Suddenly we were joined by an adolescent boy and I thought, yes, it had been too good to be true.

He spoke impeccable English with a strong American accent. He wanted to know where we were from. We were sick and tired of vultures, but knowing that very few South Africans stopped here, we made him guess. In faultless German, he guessed that we were German, in Spanish he guessed we were from Spain and, believe it or not, in Dutch he asked whether we were from the Netherlands.

I began to see the young man in a different light. His name was Haman and when I told him about South Africa, he wanted to learn Afrikaans immediately. "Goeiemiddag" and "dankie" soon rolled over his lips.

He offered his services as guide. Here it came . . .

"We don't have money."

"I don't want anything. I just want to show you my place."

We were surprised, to say the least. And so Haman led us through the streets to the Djingwerelser mosque, one of the oldest in Africa, past the ruins of the houses of the first three Europeans that had set foot here. The first, Gordon Laing, a Scot, didn't make it back to Europe, while the second, René Caillé, a Frenchman, and the third, Heinrich Bart, posed as Arabs and thus survived to tell their respective tales.

We visited the museum and had tea with a Touareg, while Haman kept up a non-stop conversation about his world. In spare moments we taught him Afrikaans. We had grown to like the boy. He arranged for us to sleep at the police station, where we "would be safe". We invited him for a meal we would be preparing ourselves. It was clear, however, that he was unused to our rich food and he merely nibbled at our Western delicacies.

When at last we left Timbuktu, he was there to bid us farewell. We threw our backpacks on the Land Rover and fumbled for a tip. He smiled, shook his head and put a silver Touareg cross in each of our hands.

"Haman," we suddenly heard behind us.

We turned and saw a tall, lean, kaftaned man standing on the veranda of the Algerian embassy.

"My pa," he said in perfect Afrikaans before he left.

A man must have papers

I met him at a wine tasting. Pompous, self-righteous people have always brought out my wilful side, and in the thick of things, with everyone sniffing and gargling and oohing and aahing, I lit my pipe. The shocked silence and the reaction of the wine master made me get up. As I was leaving, a man diagonally in front of me got up too, took out a long, thick cigar, lit it and, blowing clouds of smoke over the room with relish, walked out next to me.

It was the beginning of a lifelong friendship. He learned his first Afrikaans from me, one evening as we lay snuggled behind each other's backs beside a fire in the icy Clanwilliam cold. His first words were "hensopper" – hands-upper – and "hanskakie" – joiner.

At the age of eleven, he had fled with his parents during the Bay of Pigs invasion. For ten years his father, once wealthy, had swept the streets of Miami. Their identity documents had said "alien". Carrying frozen carcasses, bags of cement and bricks had given him the financial means to study after hours. With a prestigious qualification to his name, his new country had offered him citizenship. That blue passport with the eagle was his pride and joy. He was no longer an alien.

A South African girl had caused him to find a home away from home here, and Africa had won his heart. He and I travelled all over this southern land. From West Coast to East Coast, from forest to desert, but one thing was forbidden – to cross the red line in South-West, for he was a Cuban and I was a Boer. For three months every year I left to make war against the young men of the country of his birth. On my return we would light a cigar, pour a shot of Havana rum, and then he would ask: "How are you?"

But the war passed, and my passport allowed me to cross more borders. We decided to cross the red line together.

We approached the Angolan border post at Ruacana, planning to enter this country officially for the first time. In contrast with the Namibian side, the border post of the former Portuguese colony was shabby. The gate consisted of logs that were painted red and white and rested on two forty-four gallon drums. A tattered Angolan flag hung limply in the hot air. A camouflaged man, wearing Adidas sneakers and brandishing an AK, emerged from a shabby tent and stopped us. We were denied entry. Even requests and explanations in Spanish were turned down scornfully. Neither Boer nor Cuban was welcome in the country.

We turned the 4x4 west, and followed the Kunene River, passing the monuments commemorating the Dorsland Trek and the graves at Swartbooisdrif. It was hard, rugged country, with makalani palms and ana trees on the river banks and rocky desert and barren mountains to our left. Clearing the way and driving cautiously took a team effort. The heat was stifling, but in the evenings when the sun had drowned itself in the west and the fire was blazing, we spoke about friendship and adventure.

We were deep in Kaokoland before we realised that the Cuban had lost his identity.

Somewhere in the struggle along impassable roads, through dongas, while changing wheels or clearing roads, he had lost his passport, his identity document, his South African resident's permit, his driver's licence and R2 000 in cash. After we had turned everything upside down, we realised that the stuff wasn't merely gone, but to hell 'n gone – for where in that desolate rocky desert did one even begin to look? It was as if my friend had suddenly diminished in size. Not even a light-hearted, "Just think – somewhere there's a filthy rich American Himba with a South African resident's permit," could brighten up the grim, pale face.

We had to go back – the "alien" and I. Hundreds of kilometres were covered in silence. I was exasperated – our adventure had been cut short and nothing I tried could coax the man out of his complete silence. He acted like an automaton. At the American embassy in Windhoek I had to do the talking – he couldn't even remember his wife's date of birth. I was questioned and he was questioned and with typical American efficiency a few hours later he was in possession of a brand-new passport, eagle and all. The battle had been won, I thought, but after a few beers and further efforts at light-heartedness, I realised that the Cuban would only feel at ease again once he was back on South African soil.

It was late at night when we sped across the border on the Botswana-Kalahari route. I was tired, and the danger of animals on the road made me decide to stop and pitch camp. He got out of the bakkie like an old man – I searched for wood and made a fire. He stood around aimlessly. I let him be. We were both a little crusty. Was this the end of a friendship? Of sticking together through good times and bad?

In silence I fetched a folding chair and placed it next to the fire. He sat down. The chair collapsed under his weight. He landed flat on his big arse in the Kalahari sand. He looked up at me dejectedly.

And then we burst out laughing.

Judging a book by its cover

First I have to describe Darryl Martincich. Darryl is big and tall. His light brown hair is long, curly and unkempt. His beard is ragged. The fly of his jeans is kept together with a length of twine. His canvas shoes are worn. His oversized red jersey is threadbare and loose on his large frame.

Darryl lives on the stoep at the Sentra and takes a bath once a week in the police cells. Darryl doesn't smell good. Darryl isn't stupid – he just thinks slowly.

"It's Mandrax, meneer, luckily I gave up the stuff."

Darryl doesn't have a job. He used to be a turner in the air force at Valhalla in the days of National Service. Darryl's family in Brackenfell don't want him any more. Darryl is forty. He looks after the street children of Paarl Mountain. Darryl doesn't beg – the town looks after him. He's allowed to read in the library. ("Meneer, they spray the air around me with a can.")

The Protea cinema allows him to watch movies for free. Komma-weer Café gives him breakfast every morning – he gives it to the street kids in turn.

And every day, winter or summer, Darryl walks along Main Street looking for a job. He finds many things, but never a job.

"Meneer, a man must have a job."

"Can you lay bricks?" I asked him.

"Ja, meneer. I used to help meneer Laubscher build."

"There's a section of wall I want built. See you tomorrow."

"Right, meneer."

And Darryl and I built a wall. I had been conned before and we agreed on piecework payment.

"It's a small piece of wall, about four metres long and two metres high. I supply all the materials and equipment, and you build. Once everything is finished and I'm satisfied, I'll give you R800."

"Right, meneer, a man must have a job."

And Darryl built. After the first week the foundations had been laid – but he had used in excess of seven bags of cement and about a ton of gravel. Every morning at eight Darryl was

163

on the job and he began to build. He built until nine at night. I brought out gas lamps. My wife said people with brain damage often concentrate on the thing they are doing and forget about everything else. Darryl didn't even take a lunch break. My wall was coming along and after another two weeks it was as high as my head. It was sturdy. Ordinary cement had become concrete.

"Thank you, meneer, it's so nice to have a job."

And then he began to plaster, or should I say we did, because in the evenings after work I had to hold the planks and the gas lamps and he daubed, and bags and bags of cement were used. After a while I was standing knee-deep in dagha.

"Hell, it's nice to be working again, meneer."

I put in leave for Friday. "We must finish now, Darryl."

"Right, meneer."

On Friday afternoon we stepped back and studied his handi-work. It was a neat piece of work.

"Darryl, you have more than earned your money."

"Thank you, meneer, it was good to have a job again."

"Now, Darryl, we must deposit the money into your account."

"My what, meneer?"

"Your account. You can't leave this much cash lying around."

"I don't have one, meneer."

"Then we must open one for you. Let's do it right now."

But first I have to describe myself, especially when I have been plastering on a Friday afternoon. I am big and tall, my light brown hair is long and curly. My beard is bushy. My jeans are torn at the knees, my canvas shoes covered with plaster. I am wearing the large, loose red jersey my mother knitted for me. I didn't use That Man this morning. I live at 91 Main Street and I have a job.

We had scarcely passed through the doors of the bank when security stopped the two bums in their red jerseys.

"Can we help?"

"We want to open an account," I answered.

164

The man looked at us and gave a shitty smile. Darryl was smiling from ear to ear. I sidestepped security and headed in the direction of Management Services.

"Where do you think you're going?" The man plucked at my red jersey.

"I want to see the manager. We want to open an account."

A pretty bank lady appeared. Darryl was smiling from ear to ear.

"Menere?"

"We would like to see someone who can help us open an account. We have R800 and we'd like to open an account."

"We don't open that kind of account, meneer," she said.

"Bloody hell, lady, we're not asking for a loan – we want to give you money to keep for us," I lost my temper. "I want to see the manager."

She beat a retreat. We were big and red and I saw from the corner of my eye that security had called in reinforcements.

From an enclosed office came a little man and I suddenly realised that if we wanted to pass through the first enemy line, I would have to pull rank.

"I am Professor Bakkes of the University of the Western Cape and I would like to open an account for the man who works for me."

And the man gave a shitty smile and Darryl smiled from ear to ear.

Once we were seated, I explained the situation – of Darryl, who had worked for me and slept on the stoep at Sentra and wanted to place his money in safekeeping and draw R30 now and again.

"I have a job," I heard Darryl say from the side.

The man looked annoyed as he produced a form.

"Name?" he asked Darryl.

"Darryl Martincich."

"ID?" Darryl brought out a weathered book.

"Address?"

"But I've told you the man sleeps on the stoep at the Sentra!" I burst out.

"I've got a job," Darryl said.

"Telephone number?"

"Hell's teeth, didn't you listen to his circumstances?"

"But the man must have an address before we can open an account for him," the little man said.

"OK, let me explain to you exactly what we have come here for. I am Johan Bakkes. I live at 91 Main Street. My telephone number is 082-***-****. My bank account number is 7283***. I want to close my account and transfer my home loan to another establishment. Cash in my investments and . . . fuck you!"

And Darryl Martincich smiled from ear to ear.

"I've got a job," he said.

Headstrong

You could see that the little yellow half-caste was pissed off as he came walking towards us. He had a headstrong kind of walk. His white customs uniform gave him even more confidence as he looked us up and down.

I have crossed a lot of borders, but African border posts always get my stomach in a knot – and not because I feel guilty about anything. Except for a jerry can of whisky for Zimbabwean friends, I have never tried to smuggle anything through. I'm sorry, I'm lying – one day I limped through the Kazangula border post with rolls of Zim dollars hidden in my veldskoens.

The five of us had been waiting on the Botswana side of the Parshalt border post since six o'clock that morning. We were dirty and fed up with travelling. We were on our way home after a two-week visit to the Matetsi valley in Zimbabwe and a stop at Chobe, with its profusion of elephants. We had proceeded through Botswana with caution, for while we had been in the bush, our security forces had taken out ANC targets in Gaborone. In other words, white South Africans were being regarded with extreme suspicion.

The customs fellow was the same one who had dealt with us two weeks earlier, when we had been very arrogant as we had passed through, our adventure still ahead of us. The man had been irritated then, and I realised that he was out to get us now. Piet, Gerrie and I had been in Botswana numerous times, but it was the first time for big Hennie Palm and my younger brother Chrisjan, barely eighteen years old.

"Have you got anything to declare?" the man asked formally in colonial English. The Tswanas in the southern regions speak Afrikaans, so I knew he was being full of shit. I was in a hurry, however, because if the doctor had his calculations right, I would be a father in two weeks' time.

The main purpose of our visit had been to investigate the possibility of establishing a guided hiking trail in the Matetsi hunting area in Zimbabwe. A friend, Dan Landrey, had the concession, but the bush war, newly ended, had discouraged tourism and we had given an undertaking to bring South African tourists there, if it was economically feasible.

Grimly the customs man ordered us to unload all our paraphernalia from the Land Rover. We had nothing to hide, so with difficulty we untied the ropes and everything was lined up next to the vehicle. The man took his time – clearly he just wanted to mess us around. The entire proceedings took place in English. And then, right at the bottom of Chrisjan's backpack, in the pocket of a dirty pair of shorts . . . the rotten molar of a zebra! Ceremoniously the tooth was placed to one side. The side pocket of Hennie Palm's backpack yielded two yellowed warthog teeth. These were portentously arranged next to the zebra tooth. I knew at once that this meant trouble. I can tell the difference between mud and shit, and this was certainly not mud.

Our visit to the Matetsi had been a wonderful experience. Armed guides had accompanied us on foot through dense mopane bush and across the flood plains. A game paradise with herds of sable antelope grazing unconcernedly around us and leopards dashing out of the dry riverbed. Elephants tore at the mopane trees a short distance from us and angry lions prowled around the fires in the evenings. We felt far removed from the wars raging all over the southern tip of Africa. The stars were dazzling and bright, friendships were good and no unexpected flares stuffed up the atmosphere.

I realised I had to try and save the situation. "We came from Zimbabwe and picked this stuff up in the veld," I explained in broken English. Chrisjan and Hennie were summarily accused of importing and exporting game trophies – we were astounded! With a self-indulgent little laugh the customs man ordered the three "innocent" people to remain behind at the border post, while he – the "prosecutor"– and the "guilty" parties would head back to the Mahalapye police station along the dreadful dirt road. Not even an attempted bribe could save the situation.

Judah offered himself instead of Benjamin, for I was certainly not going to allow my little brother to be taken into the unknown alone. Under loud protest from our "prosecutor" I got into the Land Rover as well and just pretended not to understand English. Piet's last words, "We'll walk to the South African border post and fly in an attorney for you," were a slight consolation.

It was Saturday morning and there was a queue at the charge office following the previous night's murder, drinking, rape and killing sprees. We had to get out of there quickly. The border post would be closing at four that afternoon and my wife was on the verge of giving birth. But Africa has no regard for time and for us white South Africans they had no time. While charge sheets were being prepared, I rushed to the offices of Nature Conservation and as self-appointed advocate for the defence, I tried to swot up the nature conservation laws of Botswana. I realised immediately that we were buggered, because the law clearly stated that no natural objects or remains could be taken across the border without a permit. I had known that anyway.

An African jail seemed to be the inevitable destination of my younger brother and my friend Palm.

By the time our case was heard, it was two o'clock in the afternoon. Our customs official had been there the entire time. I could see, however, that the leisurely pace of the African bureaucracy, of which he was part, was taking its toll. He was fed up himself with the snail train which he had so industriously helped set in motion.

The case just before ours involved a mass murderer who had left a string of corpses behind him, stretching from Tanzania to Botswana. There were two spectators, who listened to the hearing, the guilty verdict and the passing of the death sentence apathetically. When the men from the south took the stand, however, the room was soon packed with vociferous spectators. A lynching mob, I thought. Big Hennie, dazed, and Kleinboet stood side by side, dirty and barefoot, listening to the charges against them.

The magistrate was a dissipated English colonialist in half-frame spectacles – barring a cotton wool wig, we might as well have been in a British court. Not that there was anything wrong with the man's legal knowledge, for the situation was summed up quickly. "How do you plead?"

"Guilty, your honour," they spoke in unison.

"How much money do you have?"

"Twenty pula, your honour," I shouted from the audience, knowing that it was truly the only money we had left.

"The court fines you the sum of thirty pula," we heard, and "Bam!" the gavel slammed down before I could appeal.

Though jailtime was no longer a reality, we remained stranded, for the banks would not open before Monday, the border gates would close shortly and we didn't have enough money to pay the fine.

Dejectedly we stood around and considered the possibility of selling our clothing and watches. The yellow half-caste came pushing through the crowd, heading towards us, the wilfulness no longer evident in his posture. Pressing a ten-pula note into my hand, he said in faultless Afrikaans: "Kom, laat ons ry" – Come on, let's go.

African roads

The road through Botswana is an open one. From Kasane all the way to Nata it is straight. You can sit back and put your foot down. But it's important to watch the bush around you, because nothing prevents an elephant from heedlessly crossing the road.

An African road can yield a variety of surprises. A wild dog trooping across the road out of the blue with a pack of young ones; a beautiful leopard at the roadside, trampled to a pulp by a large truck; a vehicle lying on its roof, the cab and the driver crushed, and the elephant dying somewhere in the bush on its own; now and then a corrupt policeman, trying to supplement his meagre government salary; two young girls hitching a ride somewhere . . .

I was enjoying the drive. It was early morning and Heino's voice blared in the tape recorder, making the road shorter. A cold beer between my knees. I was happiest like that. The bakkie cruising along the byways and my thoughts were doing exactly the same. A microbus overtook me. As they passed, I noticed the bright red, green and yellow headgear of a group of Rastas – they waved, smiling broadly. I waved back amiably – this is a happy road, I thought.

A while later I saw that the microbus that had passed me earlier had pulled over. The Rasta men, with long hair and dark glasses, were standing around. I saw puffs curling into the morning air. It was clearly a smoke break. Saluting them, I sped past.

A stop beside an African road can lead to interesting encounters. A passing traveller, stopping to enquire about possible car trouble, might stay for a braai and a beer; a bush artist might come walking out of the veld to display his wares; a Himba chief with an injured leg might come to ask for medicine.

One evening in the dark, we pulled off the road somewhere in Zambia. It was the only clearing we were able to find in the dense bushes. We were tired and made camp. The next morning we realised the clearing was actually a corn field, and with our truck and the pitching of our camp, we had done irreparable

173

damage. The next moment the farmer was standing there with a tray of coffee, apologising that he hadn't come out to welcome us the night before – he'd been afraid we might be Renamo soldiers . . .

The Rasta men's roadside gathering made me crave a Jamaican cocktail. I decided to stop under a large baobab, where I took a leak and laced a can of Coke with a touch of rum. It was a lovely day. As I took the first sip, the microbus pulled in next to me in a cloud of dust, and seven men jumped out.

"Hey der, mon," said one.

"Ah, breaking da fast, mon."

And we joked around a little. They were on their way to Gaborone for a celebration. It was still 800 kilometres away. I pushed a Bob Marley tape into the recorder and poured a few shots to the tune of "No Woman No Cry". The men were in high spirits and offered me some hashish. I drew deeply and the sweet aroma hung peacefully between us. I gave them a friendly reminder not to overdo things and cautioned the driver to keep a cool head – it was a long drive.

On departing, I uttered a veiled warning to my new friends: "If you find my bakkie on its roof, it's yours to inherit."

"Ah mon, we've got nuttin', but what's ours is yours."

I took my leave. Did the road seem even straighter, I wondered with a smile as they passed me a while later with fists in the air.

The first bend in the road is just before Sowapan. In the middle of a herd of cattle the crumpled bus lay on its side. The police had already arrived from Nata. Seven heaps were lined up at the roadside, covered with blankets.

I stopped. Underneath a shrub beside the road lay a brightly coloured cap.

I picked it up and placed it next to them. "I didn't want to be an heir today, mon."

Where the hell is Mombolo?

And in the long grass Wynand Burger fell to his knees. He ran his hand across the weathered gravestone:

Hier rust mijn geliefde Echtgenoot en Vader
Pieter van der Smit
Welzalig hij wiens zonden zijn vergeven . . .

Here lies my beloved Husband and Father
Pieter van der Smit
Blessed is he whose transgression is forgiven . . .

Next to him old Abraham took off his tattered hat and knelt painfully beside the grave; tears rolled down the wrinkled old cheeks as Ina began to pray. And somewhere under the hot Angolan sun history came full circle as the descendant of the Dorsland trekker – who had left – and the descendant of the Makvolk (tame folk) – who had stayed – embraced each other . . .

Now we're buggered, I thought anxiously as I clung for dear life to the wheel of the Land Rover and crawled up the pass in the lowest gear. Next to me yawned the abyss and I had to put my foot down to get over the next rocky ledge. If we stalled now, it would be the end . . . But the powerful engine rose to the occasion and, bouncing and jostling, it hauled the Conqueror trailer up the heights.

"Where the hell is Mombolo?"

This adventure began for us in a bar in Stellenbosch months before. Brother Marius, Franz Marx, Francois van Wyk and Nicol Stassen over a meal at Terrace.

"Some descendants of the Dorsland trekkers want to go to Angola. They want to see where their relatives once lived. What there is left to see. Graves . . . Perhaps kykNET will be interested. A pilgrimage, and it could be about the war as well . . . landmines and tourist opportunities," Marius remarked.

"We're coming too," it came in unison. I think it was the wine.

The next time we were together (unfortunately minus Franz – a hitch with *Egoli* had forced him to stay) it was at Swartbooisdrif on the Kunene in Kaokoland.

The Dorsland or Thirstland trek – a terrible chapter in the history of the Afrikaner people. Of stubbornness and division, of heroism, sorrow, love, death, recovery and starting over, but always the everlasting trek to the horizon.

Why had they left everything that was good and safe and in working order, packed their wagons and trekked into the wilderness? On this journey into hell, the historians say, families died of "Thirst", those who reached Lake Ngami in Botswana were exterminated by the "Fever", and the few that remained kept forging ahead . . .

Gustav Preller, in an effort to explain this phenomenon, quoted an old Trekker: "A spirit in our hearts urged us to trek. The reason for this desire was not to be understood. Our homes were peaceful and comfortable. We did not object to the government of our country, nor to taxes. Neither was it because of religion. But a driving spirit to trek was in our hearts, and we ourselves did not understand what could be the rousing cause of it . . ."

The descendants of the Dorslanders gathered at Swartbooisdrif. From here a convoy of thirty modern counterparts of the ox wagon, under the leadership of Trek Commandant Faan van der Merwe, would venture into Angola – where the Dorsland trekkers had at last decided to settle. But fifty years later, when the Portuguese government began to suppress their language and religion, they packed their wagons once again and moved back. To nothing; to start all over again.

Over a glass around a camp fire I studied my fellow trekkers. They had an "otherness" about them. An otherness that would endear them to me during the next twenty days, but an otherness that made them so different that I wished I could be like that too.

To them we were also different – the Land Rovers decorated like Christmas trees with sponsors' stickers – the "TV" that would surely only be in the way on this sacred journey – or so they thought.

We crossed the border at Omahenene/Calueque. I was entering Angola officially for the first time. Faan formed a laager somewhere in the mopane bush late in the afternoon. We pitched camp with great caution because not even a Dorsland trekker trifled with landmines. Giel and his two daughters made their camp under an ana tree while the sun was disappearing in the west. The fires burned high and people made the rounds from one outspan to the next. Dominee Kobus, a Dopper, led the evening devotions. A Reformer myself, I jokingly suggested to Dominee Alberts that we should branch out on our own.

And then the nightmare began – Angolan highways! At Cahama we got onto the tar. Say that again . . .? In Angola you avoid the tar, because a tarred road is no more than a big donga. Either the tanks have ripped up the tar, or a landmine or bomb has blasted a crater in it. And, remember, in no African dictionary does the word "maintenance" appear, and the African bush will reclaim – given enough time. It was dreadful, but amid blood, sweat and protesting vehicles, the convoy at last reached Lubango (formerly Sá da Bandeira).

We moved up the Huíla plateau and suddenly we might as well have been in the Bronkhorstspruit or Ermelo district – Highveld, and avenues of blue gum trees in a place known as Humpata. This was the location of the Dorslanders' first Angolan encampment. There was a respectful silence as their descendants formed a laager on the farm Jamba – the erstwhile family farm of the Angolan Van der Merwes.

For two days we visited various farms and places. The monument that was erected in the fifties was repaired and a new plaque unveiled. But this was not the end, because somewhere to the north, in the tall grass, at a place called Mombolo, there was a final appointment.

"But where the hell is Mombolo?" Not even on a detailed map of Angola did the name appear. With W.A. de Klerk's book *'n Swerwer op die sonpad* in his hand, Faan said: "We'll find it."

Only thirteen vehicles finally toiled down the Serra de Chella – God's Window, my arse! I had never experienced anything like it – never negotiated a pass like that one! It seemed as if the earth was falling away in front of us . . .

At the bottom we travelled through the bush, and suddenly, there was the Namib desert and then Namibe (the former Moçâmedes): a small town with its own unique atmosphere – Angola's Swakop. Amid the devastation, I could picture the good times of the Portuguese era. As a special welcome to Afrikaner visitors, a sign proclaimed ". . . elkom".

And then the fun and games began, for now we were travelling along the coast to Benguela and Lobito. If you have ever come down Van Zyl's Pass in Kaokoland, and can imagine doing it the other way round, with an ascent lasting for 160 kilometres, then you probably understand what I mean. In the meantime the "TV" wanted their "shots". It was 4x4 at its best, through the most beautiful countryside. The scenery took our breaths away. At times we might have been in Morocco, at other times in Tanzania or Malawi.

"But where the hell is Mombolo?"

Our search became an adventure in itself. We slept among landmines and derelict tanks and drove along the most atrocious roads. At a place called Londuimbali seven vehicles broke away and the rest of us continued northward on a two-track road with wooden bridges and dongas. The others had to get back home – Mombolo had broken their backs.

After two more days of drifting, with De Klerk's book as our guide, koppies and mountains began to make sense: "En daar, meteens, was voor ons 'n kom wat golwend in alle rigtings strek, tot waar dit deur die toppe van blou berge afgebaken word" – And suddenly a valley lay in front of us, undulating in every direction, until it ran out against the peaks of blue mountains. And Faan van der Merwe had a wide grin on his face.

179

I don't think the people of Mombolo often saw white people and definitely not that many in one day. I'll never forget how the little ones fussed over Willem Marais' one-year-old baby. Nico, our Portuguese-speaking travelling companion, asked about graves and ruins, but was met with blank, open-mouthed stares. Then suddenly a very old man spoke: "My basies, ek is Abraham en ek praat Hollands" – My young masters, I am Abraham and I speak Dutch. In the middle of nowhere a man spoke my language!

And Abraham with his kierie led us up the koppies and in the tall grass Wynand Burger fell to his knees in front of his grandfather's gravestone and his wife prayed.

And I stepped aside, but I truly understood their "otherness", because I too have in my heart a driving spirit to trek, nor do I myself understand what could be the rousing cause of it!

The professor and the pin-up girl

I first saw her in Foschini in Zeerust and I knew. She was the one that I wanted.

It's interesting how these things happen. That look across a crowded room. And your eye catches her looking back across the heads of the other people. Immediately the heart starts pumping chocolate. When you look again, she's no longer there. Bewildered, you push people out of the way, but she's gone. It was an illusion. It's better that way, because if she'd remained there, you might have made your way through the people unnoticed, glass in hand, and started a conversation somewhat breathlessly. Ten to one you would have talked nonsense. If she had continued to smile coyly, you might have invited her for coffee, and over coffee you might have turned on the flirtation taps, and she might have continued to smile coyly. That smile might have taken you to the pulpit like a bullet. And before you knew it, she might have been saying: "Don't drive so fast."

Or: "Don't drink so much."

Or: "The music is too loud."

Or: "Were we supposed to have gone this way?"

But when I saw her, neatly dressed in a tailored suit, her blonde hair long and wild, I knew she was absolutely perfect. "No" was never an option.

I was going to be forty in two days' time. I had a wife and children. Ten of us were spending a weekend in Central Botswana, celebrating my coming of age. My wife was optimistic that, with the advent of this new stage in my life, I would at last say farewell to puberty.

On a man's fortieth birthday the breakfast menu does not feature bacon and eggs, but something considerably stronger, especially in the company of ten friends who are making the most of the frivolous occasion. It was opening time at Zeerust, where we had stopped to take a leak and top up the vehicle with fuel.

And there she was. I realised immediately: How foolish that we were men only – this woman had to come along. I walked into the shop . . .

She gave me a look but didn't say a word. Not even "No".

"How much is she?" I asked the shop assistant.

"No, sir, only her clothes are for sale."

"What! And have her stand here buck naked for everyone to stare at? R250, and you keep the clothes," I offered.

And so, at age forty, I walked down the Main Street of Zeerust carrying the naked figure of the perfect woman under my arm.

Pop's first trip with the professor was to Botswana. Passportless, in pieces, and naked. Pottie had the lower limbs, my father, aged seventy, was happy with the torso. Eugene had her head under his arm. Schalk and Ricardo an arm each.

I like to travel on my own – I mean without another soul. Then the open road and its byways belong to me. The music is loud and there is a refreshment between my knees.

The moment another soul gets into the passenger seat, my constitution tells me I can't think only about myself any longer. But if there's no room in the bakkie, then there's no room – not even for a hitchhiker.

That is why, when I hit the road alone, Pop sits up very straight beside me, dressed nowadays in an old Fapla uniform, bandana and dark glasses.

We head for the wide horizons and Pop doesn't say:

"Don't drive so fast."

"You're drinking too much."

"The music is too loud."

"Were we supposed to have gone this way?"

To tell the truth, she says bugger all. I suspect she smiles on the inside. All that standing around in Foschini in Zeerust must have been boring.

Pop has her own passport, her own photograph, a name (Pop Bakkes), all of it real. Only the signature I forged, because she had writer's cramp. Crossing the border usually results in raucous laughter, which breaks the tension. At Noordoewer I once offered her passport to Stephni Stone of the Clanwilliam Art Gallery. Stephni had let her own one lapse. I swear it would have worked, but Stephni was afraid Pop would raise loud objections.

One day I had a drink or two in the pub at Maltahöhe. Pop was looking after the car. It was sweltering, and the pampelmoeses were flowing. Suddenly a stern Nama appeared: "Sir, I think the madam is very hot now – please stop drinking or invite her in!"

The car guards at Joe's Beerhouse in Windhoek don't look after the bakkie any more. "The madam can do it."

I must admit, when the road is long, solitary and lonely, I have been known to ask Pop how she's doing. She just smiles on the inside. Zeerust was boring.

Pop has only one disadvantage. When she sits, she sits. Lifting her out of the bakkie is accompanied by arms falling off, wig shifting and a logistical schlep in general. Pop therefore ruins any possibility of that chocolate look across a busy room leading anywhere. There's no room to take the "new" illusion for coffee – and I'll be damned if I'm willing to put Pop on the back of the bakkie.

Once I was pushing on to the desert through the Khomas Hochland via Spreetshoogte. Pop sat back, laughing happily. I alternated the Windhoek Specials with a shot of Pott rum. Not another soul was on the road. Namibia had had widespread rains. The grass stood green and tall. The weather was still changeable and there was a threatening dampness. For supper, Pop and I were planning to feast on Apfelstrudel with Moose at Solitaire, then enjoy a late-night drink at Uschi Blaauw's at Maltahöhe and then to take a nap somewhere at the side of the road before Helmeringhausen. We would refuel at Bethanie the next day.

Bethanie? Suddenly I remembered that Anna had grown up in Bethanie. Anna and Koos van Dyk from Paarl. At Solitaire there is reception and I phoned Koos, just to say I'd be travelling through Anna's hometown the next day. Believe it or not, they were also on their way the next day. There and then we arranged a meeting. We calculated it would be somewhere between Grünau and Noordoewer.

I don't know whether it was the Pott rum, the Windhoek Special or Pop's nagging but the next morning I had a hell of a headache. I felt frazzled and rotten. Not even a gin & tonic at the Goageb Hotel could get me back on track. It was hot and I was barefoot in my Kenyan robe. Pop looked austere in her Fapla uniform and dark glasses.

Nevertheless, I was looking forward to the unforeseen meeting with Koos and Anna here on the open plains of Namibia. I began to prepare for the stop and the visit. Stopping beside the road is an old South-West tradition. You stop and you visit. I put a beer or two on ice. I broke the dried sausage into bite-sized pieces and took out a packet of crisps.

At Grünau there was a message on my phone.

"Where are you? We've crossed the border." And I knew we should be meeting up after another 50 kilometres or so. I selected a tape on which Heino sang the "Suidwes-lied". I didn't know about them, but I was in no particular hurry. I knew that because they had been born and bred in Namibia we would at least be unloading the tables and chairs here on the open plain.

And just as I had thought, thirty kilometres from Grünau the two bakkies sped past each other! We flashed, waved and came to a stop about a kilometre apart. I turned, drove back and stopped on the opposite side of the road. I hurried to get out, beer in hand, and just about fell upon Koos, who was struggling to get out of his own bakkie. It was so good to see them. But Koos wasn't his usual genial self. Anna remained in the car. I greeted her through the window.

"Are you in a hurry?" I asked.

"Yes. Ma's waiting for us. Nice to see you. Goodbye."

And they were on their way. I was left standing in the middle of nowhere, holding an ice-cold beer. And I wondered whether it had been the Kenyan kikoi – they don't know me well enough, I realised.

Anna: "Jirre, Koos, the man's got a strange woman in the car."

Koos: "Can't be, Anna, he went by too quickly. Look, he only managed to stop after a kilometre."

Anna: "Koos, I'm telling you. What do I say to Nanna? We'll say hello, and then we're leaving immediately. I really don't know how I'm going to handle this thing when I get back to Paarl!"

And as they were driving away, Koos probably said: "The old bastard!"

Heavy as lead

It was after the third rum that he told me.

"I have a brother and I'm really tired tonight, but the story has to be told. Cornel was the middle child – about two and a half years my junior. Deon was too young to understand.

"Growing up among the other miners' children taught me to survive. If Rassie wasn't carving up his desk in class and setting the sawdust alight, Whitey would grab the teacher by his collar and shake him till his cigarettes fell out, or Parra would pull out his knuckle-duster and with 'Today I'll fuckin' kill you,' he would slash open someone's cheekbone. We had to stand our ground and get out alive.

"My defence strategy was simply to be better. To be the cleverest, the best sportsman, the hero of the school. It made me untouchable. I protected Deon. He was the youngest, after all. Cornel was different. He dreamed of more beautiful, better places. 'Our artist,' Pa always said. He escaped from reality with a book or an LP on the turntable. I was so busy trying to be the best that his silent suffering passed me by.

"Our annual escape was to the seaside. It was only when we reached Franskraal that we felt safe in the family circle. Then we would take our fishing rods and Pa would clamber over rocks with us and teach us about the sea and about being free. Deon was too small.

"Life went on with its twists and turns. I was successful. Cornel remained the dreaming poet and muddler, living under the shadow of 'If only you were more like Ouboet'. Perhaps things got too much for him. Finding a release in drinking probably softened the blow of my reproaches ('You're hurting Pa and Ma!').

"When Pa's terminal illness was diagnosed, my material success ensured that the role of pater familias fell on my shoulders. I was a survivor and could take it, but as the one who did everything right, I drove Cornel even further away from the warmth of the family circle and he revolted in silence. Deon found his way because he had always been protected.

"They found him in a shabby room. His face black and blue

after a bar fight, drowned in his own vomit, his hand reaching for the sheets of poetry that lay scattered on the floor. I was there to gather up the loose pieces of his life, to try and spare Pa and Ma the added grief.

"Between the sheets of poetry I came across a note . . . his wish was that his ashes would be scattered on the rocks at Franskraal.

"The cremation service was brief. A father doesn't cry and I was angry because I couldn't spare my parents the sorrow.

"I took the bag with his ashes home. It felt strangely heavy. I kept him in my wardrobe for the day that we would return to Franskraal. Every morning, as I put on my tie to go and take care of the people around me, Cornel was there. Pa didn't know about the bag.

"It was New Year's Eve, the bonfires were burning high. Just before eleven I took Pa aside and said: 'Let's go and say farewell to Cornel.'

"The bag was heavy. I didn't say another word, but when Pa caught sight of the bag, he straightened his hunched shoulders and said, 'Come, boy, let's go.'

"The sick old man led me across the rocks, as if I were a small boy again. And the bag got heavier all the time. We walked all the way to the spot where we used to wet our lines so many years before.

"And I said, 'Pa, this is far enough,' and the waves were pounding and the wind was flinging the spray back into our faces and I wanted to go back to the fire and I wanted to spare Pa the sorrow and I took the bag and scattered a bit of its contents without touching Cornel.

"And my father said, 'It's my child,' and he pushed his worker's hands into the bag so that his child got stuck under his nails and he tossed him into the wind and Cornel blew back against me and I tried to shake him off, but the salt spray made him cling to my clothes so that I couldn't let go of him, and I cried because I was unable to take care of everyone."

All in the mind

Damn, it felt as if I had been run over by a train! The second backpack, tied on top of mine, wasn't exactly making things easier. My father was with me and when I stopped and leaned slightly forward to ease the weight, he offered me water and anxiously enquired after my welfare. Even at thirty-three I remained his little boy. My body was finished – I was depending on my mind to carry on. But I couldn't worry about myself now, for I had a hell of a crisis on my hands. It was a matter of life and death . . .

Carol and Ollie had been together for ten years without bothering with a ring. The arrival of an offspring had, however, convinced them to legalise their union. To make the event memorable, they had wanted to go to Malawi with me.

Now Carol was on a stretcher and I was trying to get her off the Mulanje massif as quickly as was humanly possible. The Mulanje, the highest mountain in Malawi, offers a wonderful four to five-day hiking and climbing route and that was where the ten of us currently found ourselves. It was a two-day hike to the descent at the Fort Lister Gap and I *had* to get her off tonight, or she might die – her honeymoon had been ruined anyway.

One and a half days ago we had scaled those heights. It had been a hellishly difficult climb. The others had made use of bearers, but I, as stubborn as Piet Cronjé in days of yore, had insisted on carrying my own pack. If there is one thing I have always believed I can do properly, it is going into the mountains with rucksack and boots. But something was not right, for I had battled up the slopes. In the end I – the tour leader – had brought up the rear, feeling as if the Grim Reaper was about to give his inaugural speech.

This morning I had felt a bit better and had headed out first, with Carol happily on my heels. At lunch we had found ourselves at a beautiful stream with lovely pools and a waterfall cascading about four metres down.

"Carol, why don't you use the chance to wash while the others aren't here yet. I'll turn my back – Ollie's just behind us – you two could do with a bit of privacy.

But as I was turning round, she pitched headlong over the edge of the waterfall. I rushed across at the very moment that Ollie, who had just arrived, jumped in after her, screaming. Below, I pulled her broken body out from under the waterfall.

The Malawian bearers, who were taking turns carrying the stretcher, rested at regular intervals. I had to urge them on, even though I myself wanted to collapse on the spot. If your mind is right, you can do anything, I kept telling myself. Carol was seriously injured, a bandage covering a gaping hole in her head. I suspected that her nose, ankle and wrist might be broken as well. But the worst was that I didn't know what damage there might be inside her skull. Ollie's chin needed stitches. He was walking next to the stretcher, holding her hand.

It was dusk when the woeful procession arrived at the Shiwa hut. It was too dark to go down the cliffs and I called a halt. When we removed the bandages, things didn't look good. We cleaned the wounds and administered painkillers. I was dog-tired and nauseous – exhaustion, for sure. Pa and I made our beds outside. The night went by in a succession of nightmares. I broke out in a cold sweat. I dreamed of death and mayhem and my dad held his son's hand.

Day was just breaking as we tackled the descent down the Fort Lister Gap. Carol was still alive and I ran ahead, carrying my two backpacks, to arrange for immediate transport to Blantyre. Damn, I really wasn't feeling well . . . I wanted to puke, but I held it back – the other two were more important now.

The Queen Elizabeth Hospital resembled the Bath of Bethesda. Sick, near-dead and screaming people were milling about. I pushed my way through them with my casualties. I knew I had to keep a cool head, especially since Aids was a reality. At last I found a doctor. He looked even worse than the picture I had in my mind of the butcher of Belsen – apron soaked with blood and a huge pair of pliers in his hand. Diagnosis: the wounds were too old, patching could not be done.

My body was done for, but my mind was working overtime.

My people had to be treated or else flown out. It was Sunday and the next flight home was only on Tuesday. At last an American doctor at a mission hospital stitched the wounds late that night. X-rays mercifully showed no signs of brain damage.

I booked the honeymoon couple into a hotel – the rest of the team was happy enough to camp at the ninth hole of the Blantyre golf club.

And when everyone had been placed, patched, organised, fed, soothed and cared for . . . that was when I lapsed into a coma with cerebral malaria.

Barry Viljoen

I'm drowning, I realised with a shock.

The brown waters of the Bashee River churned and eddied, and I was swallowing mouthfuls of muddy water. Desperately I clung to my backpack that served as a float. I kicked fruitlessly against the current that was dragging me out to sea. Sheets of rain came pelting down mercilessly. When I managed to lift my tired head above the waves, I could barely make out the dim form of Barry, 100 metres away on the opposite bank.

Then the furious, churning water pushed me under. I was dead tired. At what exact point does everything cave in and you lose your grip on life?

I was being washed out to sea swiftly – the great mass of water was starting to roll my rucksack over and over, and me along with it. First I was up, then I was down. Today's 50-kilometre hike along the Transkei Wild Coast, struggling against the rain and a black southeaster, had drained all my reserves. If only I could cross the bloody river – food and shelter and our logistical support team were waiting on the opposite bank. What a person won't do to get into the papers, I thought desperately as the churning water pulled me under once again. We were raising funds for marine conservation and were trying to walk the entire length of the South African coast from end to end in 60 days, thus the 50 kilometres per day.

"What a shit idea!" I shouted underwater. My head broke through the surface, and the next minute an uprooted tree was on top of me. I dived down and felt the branches tearing at my shirt and tugging at my backpack, the only thing that had been keeping me more or less afloat. I lost my desperate grip on it.

It's over, I thought as I was swept helter-skelter along the bottom and out to sea . . . A walrus took me around the waist and gently rubbed my head. "Stay calm," he said and swam with me to the bank.

And so Barry Viljoen brought me back to life.

Barry Viljoen. A gentle man. A helpful man. Nothing was ever too much trouble for him. We had many adventures together. He was 20 years my senior but as tough as nails, built for discomfort, and loyal until death.

I remember a Christmas Eve in the Kaudom, with the crimson South-West sun melting in the west. Rough male voices singing "Silent Night" and exchanging handshakes instead of gifts. I remember the descent into the Ubusis kloof in the Naukluft mountains, with Barry leading terrified friends step by step down the heights. Carrying two backpacks in the Fish River canyon, when clients could no longer manage. Always a sympathetic ear for those who were hurting and feeling sad around the camp fire.

Barry, the brickmaker, who had built the wall around my house. Who one evening, while I was lying snugly in my sleeping bag, jumped with his knee on my chest and said: "You're fucking up your body. Don't! There are still many years of adventures ahead!"

Proud Barry, who, when the economy began to strangle him, headed for Lesotho to build houses there: "If I can't earn money here, I'd rather go and build houses free of charge for people who *really* need them."

And so he had disappeared from my life for a while.

The media invited me, as leader of an expedition, to a do at the Krugersdorp Lion Park. I had heard Barry was back and working at a nearby brickyard and I stopped there on my way to the function.

I noticed that the shoulder of his shabby jersey was frayed and torn. He had grown old. I told him I loved him. Would he like to join me later that evening at the Lion Park? We could talk about what was in the past and what lay ahead. Bugger these strangers and their goings-on.

It was a great party and the liquor flowed. Barry didn't come, and with a few drinks too many under my belt I hit the road late that night – back to Pretoria. At the Tarlton/Krugersdorp junction nature called urgently. I stopped, and while I was leaning with one shoulder against the bakkie, taking a leak, a car pulled up. It was Barry.

"Are you all right?" he asked.

"Yes, Ouboet, you know me. When I've been drinking, I can drive home in reverse with my eyes shut!"

"Look after yourself – there are people who need you," he said.

And that night he drove behind me for 60 kilometres, until I reached the turn-off to my home. I can still recall the way he laughed and waved as he turned and drove away.

Carol phoned the next morning. Barry had been looking forward to joining me the day before, but late in the afternoon he had collapsed with a heart attack – she didn't know about funeral arrangements yet.

He had built my wall.

Trapezium

I noticed them again when I pushed open the door of the dimly lit bar at Matjiesfontein. The bar was half-full. The smell of old wine, cigar smoke and beer-soaked wood mingled with smells and sounds from the past – lavender, gunpowder and war cries from the Anglo-Boer war. I chose a corner at the counter, from where I could observe the bar and its occupants unnoticed. I like looking in from the outside and wondering . . .

They were probably the most beautiful couple I had ever seen. They were at the far end of the bar, unaware of what was happening around them. As if they had eyes only for each other. Perhaps "beautiful" is not the right word. For her, yes. Small, delicate, with almond-brown eyes. Her short hair combed back stylishly. A black low-necked evening gown accentuated the handfuls of her breasts. Her lips, soft red, were the same colour as the long silk scarf, draped almost carelessly around her neck. Most beautiful, however, was her radiant, laughing face as she looked up at him.

To be honest, he was bloody ugly. Formally dressed in bow tie and tailcoat, he stood leaning protectively against her back. His wild mane and bushy beard did not match his neat evening attire. A conspicuous white scar began at the corner of his mouth and disappeared into his beard. When he laughed, his face was even more disfigured. I realised it was their being together that made the difference. His boisterous laugh, meant for her ears alone, and her delight in the moment made them the most beautiful people I had ever seen. And I wondered . . .

If there is one thing I find irresistible, it's a bar in the platteland. I just *have* to go in. The bar of a town is its soul. Knowledge of a lifetime can be gathered there in the space of half a day spent looking and listening. You have the choice of joining in or remaining on the outside. Every bar has its own character, though. As an outsider, you must never allow yourself to become a threat to the town and its soul

I remember walking into the khaki-clad bar of Kuruman one day. I was travelling with a sawn-off shotgun for those nights when I decided to sleep next to my bakkie at the roadside. My training made me surrender my weapon to the barman when I entered. As I ceremonially placed my traditional weapon on the counter, an arsenal of weapons from the pockets of thirty other occupants were also slammed down on the counter. I spent that evening having a braai with the town's neighbourhood watch.

My route to Matjiesfontein had taken me through the Upper Karoo. From Prieska I had travelled to Carnarvon via Van Wyksvlei, where I had vociferously cheered on the Springboks against the All Blacks in the bar with the largest collection of beer cans in the southern hemisphere. After ten o'clock tea and a game of pool with the mayor of Fraserburg, I had pointed the nose of the bakkie in the direction of the Moordernaarskaroo via Sutherland and the Roggeveld.

People who don't rush past Matjiesfontein usually make a quick detour, take a photograph of the hotel, buy a knick-knack at the post office store and carry on with their journey. That is a mistake! Matjiesfontein is a place to be explored on foot, to be looked at and felt. That was why I had decided on arrival: Tonight I'm going to spoil myself. And I had booked into the hotel.

I had taken a walk through the little town. At the chapel I had seen them for the first time – it had been one of those quick glances into the private moments of others, before turning away guiltily. She had been on the floor in front of the figure of Christ, clad in dark red, her hands folded in prayer. He had been standing behind her, arms folded, his knees against her back.

Every bar has its own ritual. Fritz Bücher's welcoming drink of Stroh in the little bar at Bronkhorstspruit; kissing the buffalo at Hectorspruit; drinking pampelmoes at Maltahöhe; the panties at Gouda and Dave Walker's "Thanks, Charlotte" in the bar at Rhodes. Those are the moments when a stranger can make himself part of the soul of a town. That's when his fellow drinkers open up and talk about . . .

"The day Willeman stormed in here and fired seven shots through the roof, because his wife . . ."

"The day my wife sent the kids in to fetch me . . ."

"The day Pedro went and hanged himself in the toilet . . ."

"The day they came to make a movie here and we were all so plastered . . ."

In a bar you can get to know people if you want to, but you can also stand back.

Except for the candles that threw flickering shadows on the walls, lighting the tables dimly, the dining room was dark. I sat down. They were sitting in a dark corner slightly behind me to the left, leaning across towards each other. These were older people. Theirs wasn't puppy love – they had come a long way and they had suffered. I was sitting reasonably close to them and with half an ear I heard their conversation coming and going. All I could really make out was a bubbling delight – they are happy, I thought. What was it that made them so obviously different? I relished the taste of the red wine with which I washed down the Karoo mutton stew. For dessert there was coffee and crystallised orange peel. I kept watching them surreptitiously. In the candlelight their faces seemed vaguely familiar. Or was it my imagination?

To help digest my dinner, I took a walk along the railway line into the Karoo night. The stars were luminous and bright. I lay down on the tracks and my eyes looked further than a person can see. The Orion Nebula had often been my direction finder at night. Six stars form the Trapezium. I drew a line through Bellatrix and Procyon to Regulus, and, yes, to my delight I found Leo to the north – a northern hemisphere galaxy that shows itself here during autumn.

The cold drove me back to the bar.

The drink I had ordered settled pleasantly in my stomach. I was happy to be a mere onlooker tonight. No ritual to make me part of the soul. Only speculation. The couple fascinating me with their body language, their talking, their laughing – unaware that I was looking in. Leo and Trapezium, I thought, and suddenly I recalled an article I had read about a visit to De Aar by the Boswell-Wilkie Circus. The trapeze artist high above the crowd, missing the bar as well as the safety net and plunging into the steel enclosure of the lions – the lion tamer charging bare-handed into the cage and keeping the terrified lions at bay . . .

When he picked her up tenderly in his arms, I noticed for the first time the wheelchair in the dark corner.

Love

I have always wondered about those mushy love songs.

Finished, fucked up, hurt, had, spent, squandered, wonderful, where, where to . . . I could probably use up the entire alphabet to describe love, if I wanted to. After all, Joan Armatrading points out that there's "more than one kind of love". True.

I am familiar with camaraderie. Men who watch your back when you lie in all-round defence during stand-to. And the rising sun is deceptive.

I once knew a stray dog that made a father of me when I was still a little boy. Food smuggled out secretly – my mother wasn't to know. In the evenings I told my father I'd be sleeping in the tree house and I held him in my arms as I slept. Then they shot him because something had been catching the sheep. And afterwards the catching went on . . . It had probably been a jackal. I never had a dog as a pet again.

At a movie I tried to hold her hand after interval. Then her dad left with another woman. I don't think she wanted to hold hands after that.

A boys' school. Rugby, bicycles and weekends off into the Magaliesberg with backpacks. We trusted blindly and jumped from cliffs into shallow pools. Trust was love.

During puberty it's not an easy thing to ask someone to go steady – in fact, it's a hell of an operation. Saving your pocket money for months, putting on your hipster bell-bottoms, asking your dad to take you to the movies. Afterwards, over coffee, she says no.

Expeditions – the possibility that you might die exists per definition, or the media and the sponsors would not be interested. An embrace ("For the jol – we'll crash and burn") when death has turned its back on you.

Japie Greyling saying: "You can shoot me, but I won't tell you where my father is." Children finally tie you down. Your own blood. Continuing the bloodline. They accept you for what you are. Without reservations. "He's my dad." Perhaps the greatest selflessness of love.

Then you run into her years later. Just like that, and it's an immediate fuck up because you no longer know *how* to love . . . And there's pain.

Easter weekend. You sit in a bar and you write the final letter, for delivery and closure. It's for survival. It's a sad letter that says how you don't know anything about love, but . . .

Then you leave and across the street there's a small church. And voices singing the most beautiful Easter hymns drown out the raucous sounds coming from the bar. And you walk into the church. And you walk straight into Love.

And the letter is posted.

Saints

She was the darling of the Argentinian citizenry. They worshipped the ground under her feet. She looked after the poor, provided schools and food. St Evita. Saintly little Eva, they called her.

Nanna, my wife, is not exactly a saint – she gives me a whole lot of grief, for the sole reason that I deserve it. She'll go to heaven, for sure, because she's had hell with me.

A clinical psychologist by profession, she did her best for twenty years to mend people's broken souls. Dazed, she returned home every day to keep the Bakkes family together.

To remain sane herself, she started to paint – the most beautiful things. Others also find them beautiful. But her Achilles heel remains the suffering of helpless people. She has a soft spot for children and old people. And animals, of course. In our yard there are four Airedale terriers. And two cats. They all have human names. They are the chosen ones. Those of us who can look after ourselves have become used to playing second fiddle.

When she turned fifty, I surprised her with a weeklong visit to Buenos Aires, as penance and birthday gift.

And the pulsating city of Evita Perón drew us in completely. Nanna blossomed. We strolled from one art gallery to the next. We visited Carlos in Carmonito and Nanna danced the tango. We bought paintings in the streets of Palermo Viejo. She loved the dog walkers of El Centro, and was delighted by the contented cats in the botanical gardens.

But the ragged children begging for alms until after midnight in Florida and Lafayette Streets dampened her joy at being there.

We joined the parade on the Plaza de Mayo, paid a visit to the gauchos in San Antonio de Areco. We bought her the most beautiful Indian jewellery, and an evening dress for a tango show. But in Recoleta we entered the Cementerio de la Recoleta and Nanna began to follow the trail of Eva Peron. From the mausoleum where she lay buried, to the Casa Rosada, to her statue in Recoleta, to the museum in Palermo Soho.

The trip was nearly over, and we decided on an Argentinian spitbraai as a farewell. In the afternoon the La Chacra restaurant had caught our eye. Our funds were low, however, and the budget stretched thin. I had a bank card, but a previous transaction had failed to clear, so we would have to be frugal and not go overboard. But it was all about the experience, I told myself.

Towards the middle of the evening we set out, all dressed up. The children, dirty and ragged, were out in the street, begging. Bedraggled Indian women with children at the breast pleaded dejectedly. The poor had crawled out of their lairs.

The menu was Spanish, as was the waiter. His attempts to describe the food only added to my confusion. At last I got hold of the wine list. It was a thick one. I paged through it, searching for the cheapest items. The French champagne section caught my eye. Hell, it's expensive, I thought. I had never tasted it, and probably never would. I ordered what my empty pocket could afford. Then I looked around me. The place was cosy, with a wonderful atmosphere. Next to us carcasses were rotating on a spit. Buses arrived and tourists were cheerfully devouring large chunks of meat. Bathed in luxury, the privileged ones laughed. And in the streets . . .

The waiter returned and from his patronising conversation, all of it in Spanish, I inferred that there was none of my cheap wine to be had. He pointed at something double the price. It's a scam, I thought. He has no time for church mice. I was becoming annoyed and searched grimly for the second cheapest – again my eye fell on the French champagne. It has never been on the cards for me, I sighed inwardly.

We Afrikaners are crazy about meat, as are the Argentinians. It was therefore important for me to get a taste of what was sizzling on the open fires. Bearing in mind my financial position, Nanna's appetite and the waiter's Afrikaans, I ordered a mixed grill for one, to be shared between the two of us.

Another bottle of wine – Nanna was getting prettier by the minute and around me the tourists were chattering. Our mixed grill for one was served on a bed of hot coals. It consisted of large quantities of all kinds of meat. After a valiant attempt, even I had to throw in the towel.

"What happens to the meat that is left?" Nanna inquired.

"I suppose they give it to the poor." I knew that was what she wanted to hear.

"I would really like to know," she persisted.

I waved to the waiter, who by this time was doing his best to avoid me and the communication gap between us. I tried my best to ask what would become of the meat on our plates. The expression on his face grew more and more puzzled.

Is it underdone? Do I want him to take it back? he seemed to be thinking, as he babbled in Spanish.

"Fuck, woman, just leave it alone."

"Did you see what it's like in the streets?" she snookered me.

I tried again. Helplessly the waiter motioned to the rear.

An elegant gentleman in tails approached.

"I'm the maître d'. Can I help?"

In English I explained my wife's problem.

He studied her attentively and with a slight bow he explained that the foodless of Buenos Aires queued at the back door at closing time and everything that was left over was distributed. The evening was saved, and I considered ordering more wine, but I realised the occasion was coming to an end. My money was finished and I asked for the bill.

While the calculations were being made, I gently berated Nanna. "You do have a way of upsetting the apple cart, you know."

She gave a saintly little smile.

"Signora." He had a bottle of Dom Perignon in his hand.

"No, fuck," I muttered. I certainly couldn't afford it. Was the waiter getting his own back?

"No, no!" I gesticulated wildly and pointed at my full stomach.

"Um Casa," he said and put the bottle in front of Nanna.

I jumped up.

"Receipto – no! No!"

The next moment the master of the house was back. "This is on the house . . . for Evita."

I looked at my wife. Was I imagining it? Was it the wine?

In the twilit restaurant she was bathed in a soft light.

For the sake of . . .

In the army we used to talk about a man being "bossies". But that was when we were talking to a civvy. When we spoke to each other, it was simply "bosbefok".

Ever since childhood I have been "bosbefok". Not like in the army, though, because in a military context you were "bossies" when you had spent too much time in the bush – in other words in the war – and you were beginning to lose your marbles. Then you were sent to Ward 22.

I'm crazy about the bush. There's no better place for me. The bush represents the freedom of nature – an escape into the wild. Please don't ask me to book into a hotel or to mope through a holiday at the seaside or to languish in a timeshare in a game reserve. On day two I'll be chewing at the curtains – a thorn in the flesh of everyone around me.

In time a man takes a woman, and if he's lucky, there'll be a cub or two. What my appendages hadn't known was that they had bought themselves a pig in a poke. Before they knew it, we were heading for the bush in the roughest way possible.

Marc was barely four months old when I took a tour group through Botswana. We were travelling in a convoy, and after a breakdown we were still on our way to Serondella on the Chobe River when darkness fell. I drove ahead in the bakkie to prepare the camp site. It was pitch-dark, the bush ominously dense. In the back of the bakkie lay Marc and his little sister, Cara, barely two years old. We had cleared a little space for them to lie, up against the cab among fridges, leaking jerry cans and other camping equipment. At one stage my wife reached back through the sliding window.

Horrified, she cried out: "The children are missing!"

That's fucking impossible, I thought, and slammed on the brakes in the thick sand.

I got out. As I walked round to the back, I imagined that the bush around me was alive in the dark. And believe it or not, the next minute I saw the trees move. Then I caught the smell. I realised we had stopped in the middle of a herd of grazing elephants!

But still – a mother's fear . . . Moments later she touched the warm little bundles amid all the equipment.

It was minus eleven degrees, the thermostat said, as I got up at dawn to boil water for coffee. Mata-Mata in the Kalahari Gemsbok Park was our gateway to South-West/Namibia. The members of the tour group lay frozen stiff in their tents, my family was under the steel canopy of the bakkie. I opened a beer to get rid of the foul taste of the previous night. After two sips the liquid froze.

With steaming Milo and a titbit for my offspring, two and four years old respectively, I woke the family, stumbled, and the hot liquid spilled over the sleeping bags and their occupants. In front of my eyes the steaming beverage congealed as it rolled across the sleeping bags.

But at an early age they learned to love the call of the fish eagle. They saw Mukurob, the finger of God, before it collapsed. They witnessed genets frolicking in the night. They could climb a Kalahari dune and play hide-and-seek with a meerkat. They knew the cheetah's eyes are streaked with tears because it can't climb a tree. And that lions going "huggh" around the camp site are not hungry, but merely curious.

It was the Christmas holidays. The family was alone. Camping idyllically on the Zambezi River, away from everyone else. While the sun was going down in the direction of Zambia, waterbuck came down to swim in the river. Elephants snooped around and lions came to call, growling. I was euphoric. In the mornings we bathed primitively in water drawn in buckets, while crocodiles watched us and we watched them. We were alone in the wilderness.

After one of these morning baths my wife stepped on the rim of the basin and fell flat on her face in the sand.

"Fuck you, this is the last time I'm ever getting out of a primitive bath to set foot in the sand."

And I saw years of pent-up rage boiling to the surface . . .

To the deep sound of a lowing foghorn and with streamers fluttering down to the quay, the *Achille Lauro* left Durban harbour. For the sake of . . . I waved at people I didn't even know. For the next few days this ship would be my allotted space.

It was ridiculously luxurious – to the point of having four meals a day. There was a nightly variety of beautiful girls executing dance steps, magicians pulling rabbits out of hats, comedians who could make the most constipated person laugh, deck games that made the voyagers even more nauseous.

And around me the endless sea.

And we cruised – the children watched movies and swam and ate and demanded more money for the coin-devouring electronic games.

And then the ship caught fire and began to sink, and because I didn't know enough about the endless ocean and was therefore unable look after my people, I was overcome by helplessness.

And when we were all safe, they asked: "Pa, when are we going to the bush again?"

Reunion

. . . and I lost control and I headed straight for Auntie Ada and there was no stopping me and I knocked her legs from underneath her so that her blue varicose veins split open. And crying, I helped the stout coloured woman to her feet. I was eleven years old.

"Sorry, Auntie Ada, I'm sorry, Auntie Ada," I mumbled between sobs and I thought: Am I about to lose *another* mother?

I had just wanted to show her how well I could drive my soapbox car. With great difficulty she had shuffled to the bottom of the hill. "Look, Auntie Ada, here I come!" I had called . . .

Now the little boy was half-dragging, half-carrying the old woman with the lacerated legs back to the house of death.

My own mother was nearly at death's door. Cancer, they had tried to explain to us two bigger ones. Matilde and Chrisjan were too young – Chrisjan couldn't even say "Ma" yet. We were living in Saldanha, and my father was immersing himself in work to escape from his own sorrow.

Auntie Ada was our second mother – she looked after everything. Had been doing so for years. "Don't worry, Johannes," she consoled me.

During the months my mother was being tormented in Wynberg Military Hospital, Auntie Ada held the fort. She couldn't help us with our school work, but every morning we got onto the bus spick-and-span. Auntie Ada's white children.

My own mother returned, but neither she nor Saldanha was ever the same again. We left for the Transvaal and Auntie Ada went back to her own children in Hopefield. We never returned.

That is how my second mother disappeared from my life.

Eleven years later. A man in a bakkie had dropped me off just outside Hopefield. With backpack and floppy hippie hat I headed into town.

It was a dismal place. The West Coast sun glinted bleakly on the limestone road. Manitoka trees leaned permanently to the southeast. Someone gave me directions.

The township lay sprawled across the sand dunes. All the houses had the same whitewashed walls and black tin roofs. People were living there. I wondered if she could possibly still be alive.

"Do you happen to know Ada Absalom?" I asked at one of the first houses.

"Yes, meneer, she lives with her children in block C over there.

"She's very old . . ." I heard as an afterthought as I continued down the dusty road.

As I walked on, children began to emerge from the houses, dancing in the wake of the hippie piper.

"House H7," someone called. It appeared that everyone in this entire dune village knew the woman. What influence could she have had on their lives?

I walked up a slope and when I reached the top, I spotted the house. From a distance I saw a hunched old woman sitting on a chair in the sun. She had her back to me. I wondered if she'd remember me – it had been so many years . . .

I pushed the gate open . . . the woman stiffened. My entourage had fallen silent and was waiting meekly at the bottom of the road.

I walked up to her and put my hand on her shoulder.

"Good day, Auntie Ada," I said.

"Good day, Johannes. You're back."

She turned around. The blind woman laughed – she laughed with tears running down her cheeks.

Dr Jan van Elfen

I was beside myself with rage and raised the hippo-hide sjambok shoulder high. I'll beat the fucking daylights out of you, was the last thought that flashed through my mind . . .

There is a book that has a permanent place on my bedside table. Eighteen years ago there were two. The Bible and *Babasorg* – Baby Care – by Dr Jan van Elfen. In those days we probably studied the Gospel according to Dr Van Elfen more ardently than that according to Matthew, Mark, Luke and John put together. Nevertheless, we weren't completely clueless. After all, Marc was our second attempt, so having raised Cara – 23 months his senior – made the research slightly easier.

The book had been a gift from my mother. In the front she had written: *To Nanna and Johannes, with love and great joy from Mamma.* I didn't quite understand the "and" and why she had underlined it three times. Nor the fact that *she*, who had raised four babies, should present *us* with a book.

I'll never forget the moment the head crowned and I saw that he had a little willie. His first cry sounded like the foghorn at Cape Columbine, and he looked like Rocky after completing twelve rounds in the ring, but he was *mine*.

Thus another little being became part of the Bakkes clan of Doringkloof, Verwoerdburg. We couldn't afford Huggies; the nappies and I went into the shower together.

When the little man said "eeeeh", we thought it might be time for No-more-cramps, when he said "ooooh", the little fellow wasn't getting enough breast, according to Dr Van Elfen . . . And so we carried on, chapter after chapter. I recall the good doctor's advice in Chapter 22, the one titled "man to man": *If your baby keeps crying at night and your wife is desperate for some rest, get out of bed and go to the baby. Feed him and walk around the room with him. If he still refuses to sleep, unlock the liquor cabinet and measure out half a teaspoon of brandy. Give it to him mixed with water and sugar, put him down and he will sleep peacefully – and so will you. The next morning your wife will tell her friends what a wonderful husband you are.*

I must say I didn't follow that advice to the letter. I used to pour myself a shot at the same time.

And so Nanna, Marc, Dr Jan and I continued up to the age of three. That was where the book ended. All that remained after that was the Bible. Deuteronomy 21, verse 18: *If a man has a stubborn and unruly son who will not listen to his father . . . then all his fellow citizens shall stone him to death.* An anonymous interpreter is reported to have said that Abraham had been willing to sacrifice Isaac, not because the Lord had ordered him to, but because Isaac had been in standard seven.

I have mentioned before that my own father didn't have a father – his father had died when he was three months old. Despite the absence of a role model, I believe he was the best. Nothing was too much trouble for him where his children were concerned. Don't get me wrong: He thrashed us when we deserved it. And we often deserved it.

Then he and I somehow lost each other temporarily. According to my mother, I developed a delayed puberty in my nineteenth year and became absolutely impossible. I'll never forget the first time I saw blind fury in my father's eyes – I think I had been shouting at my mother. I realised he was about to punch me and took to my heels. He cornered me in the garden, raised his hands, wiped across his face, turned and walked away.

It was the worst hiding I had ever received in my life. For two years we spoke only when absolutely necessary.

And today – today he's my best friend. I can share anything with him. From a beautiful piece of music to a good wine to a journey through the Dorsland. I can tell him everything – the good and the bad. He loves me.

I believe my immortality lies in my progeny, and I'm determined to be a good father to them – my father taught me how, after all. I also believe that things from the past are important for the future. I tell them about the past and the future.

One day I came across a real hippo-hide sjambok. You don't find those any more (these days they're made of plastic). It was given pride of place in my bar – something for posterity . . .

I took my children on trips. I showed them places that *I* find beautiful. I played them *my* sixties music. I gave them books that *I* had loved to read. I braaied for them every evening, because it is *my* greatest joy. If something was exceptional, I shared it with them. If Marc jumped from the railway bridge into the Berg River, it was fine – *I* had done it too. I don't understand television and computer games. Marc and I played war games with soldiers *I* had painted.

And then I lost Marc. He grew up right under my nose. He began to do his own thing, and it wasn't *my* thing, and I didn't understand.

It was the matric farewell. The man was dressed up. The girl was pretty. The evening had been carefully planned. They would be travelling to the before, the middle and the after-party by bus. The next morning he had not come home. In vain I consulted *Babasorg* – I was the only one who would benefit from No-more-cramps, I realised – and I got mad. I had made the rules, after all.

Slightly dishevelled, he stood in front of me. I was nursing a hangover myself.

"Where have you been?"

"At the matric farewell," he answered, and I saw the defiance in his eyes.

"Is this the time to come home? We've been worried sick."

"It's the end of my childhood. The grown-up world is waiting. But Pa won't understand." And he turned his back on me.

That was when I grabbed the sjambok from the bar, beside myself with rage.

"I'll teach you about being grown-up," I said and raised the sjambok shoulder high. He looked me squarely in the eye.

"You won't hit me," he said softly.

And I hit him and the sjambok made a swishing sound and he looked me squarely in the eye. And his own eyes were saying: You poor arsehole, you've never grown up yourself.

221

And I, poor arsehole, turned and knew that *now* he was gone. I still hope I can be his best friend one day, because I love him.

Dreams and realities
(A travel essay)

Who is he? What makes him roam around the dark back streets of Addis Ababa tonight? What is he looking for? He lingers in front of a closed door. A chink of light. Africa pulsating deep in the belly of the place. And then he walks in. Through the open door, past warm bodies wriggling to the rhythm of the asiska. What is a white man doing alone in the bleeding Mercato so late at night? Didn't they kill 37 people here during a march the day before yesterday? Not even ordinary people should be in these streets late at night . . .

Perhaps it would be a good thing to enter and take a look as well. Inside there is the aroma of coffee. Somewhere in a corner a beautiful woman with finely chiselled features is roasting coffee beans on a coal stove. The light is dim, the music captivating, rhythmic. A busty woman dances the asiska frenziedly, in the traditional Ethiopian way – only the breasts moving, the rest of the body filled with promise. The drums roll and the storyteller laments the death of the people of Mercato. The single-string masenko remonstrates with life. The audience, each with a pile of quat leaves, chews obliviously into the night. Occasionally someone jumps up and nuzzles one of the dancers. There's a hopeful passion – tonight we're alive . . . tomorrow?

The traveller sits in a corner, a cold Bati beer in his hand. He is eating injira, Ethiopian sourdough bread, with a hot meat smirrie. You can see he is making himself part of what is happening here. He is conspicuous – he's white, a "firangi" in their language, but he seems to fit in. He's supposed to be here – he's from Africa too.

 Ever since childhood books and music have enkindled in me a thirst to experience life. As an eleven-year-old I used to curl up in front of my dad's turntable and listen to music he had brought from far horizons, while I devoured books about strange places which my mother had thrust into my hands. And I knew any place on this globe would eventually grow too small for me.

I wanted to see what lay on the other side of the koppie, and secretly I hoped that there would be another koppie, so that I could carry on until I had seen its other side as well. The music and the books caused a few places to linger mysteriously in my mind. With names representing the unknown. Timbuktu, Katmandu, Khartoum, Calcutta, Casablanca and Cairo. Also the Sahara. And at a very young age I promised myself that one day I would go there.

But life doesn't consist of dreams alone; there's also reality. And reality caught up with me. The reality of existence. Of what has to be done. I had to study, and I did. I had to go to the army, and I did. I had to go to work, and I did. I married and had children. I had to turn forty, and I did, and I had to experience Timbuktu, Katmandu, Khartoum, Calcutta, Casablanca and Cairo and I did not . . .

At forty I was a chartered accountant, a professor and a captain in the South African Defence Force, I was the father of two beautiful children, I was the proud owner of a great many things, like cars and a house and part of a game farm, and I was successful. But I was no longer the eleven-year-old dreamer – I had not yet been to Timbuktu, Katmandu, Khartoum . . .

Dear Friends

I am writing this letter from a place called Dangla, about 85 km south of Bahir Dar. Bahir Dar – where we were first introduced to Ethiopia, its people, its churches and its Blue Nile four weeks ago.

Do you remember the Sunday in the island monastery of Kebran Gabriel on Lake Tana, where the elderly priest conducted a service especially for the four men from South Africa?

My bus stopped here at Dangla, because it is illegal to drive from Addis to Bahir Dar in a single day; no buses are permitted on the roads after dark.

I must say, tonight I really miss you. I miss the adventures and the camaraderie we shared. The post-mortem on our experiences here in Ethiopia. Taking leave of you was rather shit – with you going back to South Africa and me staying behind. I thought of all kinds of things to make being alone easier. For instance: "Hell, it's going to be nice on my own for a change. I'm fed up with travelling in style anyway."

I also had quite a few beers. I could easily have got onto that plane with you, if it hadn't been for a few things still missing in my life. Unfinished dreams. Timbuktu, Katmandu and Casablanca are already locked into my memory, and just ahead lie Khartoum, the Sahara and Cairo. Calcutta will have to wait . . .

The three days in Addis were good. I walked all over the city. Sorted out my affairs, watched the rugby between the Springboks and the French at the Hilton Hotel, went to pubs and wrote.

And then the wheels began to turn. Excited as a child, I sat down next to the driver of the dilapidated bus at half past four in the morning, my backpack loaded with gin and Game, as we set off on our way to Gonder in East Central Ethiopia.

But the bus did not leave before every possible space had been filled with bodies and luggage. Behind me sat a teacher from Humera, Tsegaye Shiferaw. He could speak a bit of English and we began an awkward conversation. Humera is in the north-eastern corner of Ethiopia, on the Sudanese and Eritrean border. He lectures in history and geography and was returning from a congress in Addis.

The journey is difficult to describe – as is the bus. At the front of the cab hung funeral wreaths and pictures of the Virgin Mary. The right front wheel (over which I was seated) was badly buckled, which meant that, whenever there was a bend in the road, the steering wheel would jump out of the hands of Hanji, our driver. The U-bolts protested with a loud clacking noise. We drove up and down mountains. At regular intervals the conductor passed out green puke bags for the passengers at the back. I kept my eyes to the front, kept pouring gin and worked up a piss.

In the process the driver laughed, ran over a dog (with my wheel) and knocked two donkeys out of the way.

I developed an urgent call of nature, but the bliksem refused to stop. I seemed to have given up smoking as well. Only once during the twelve-hour journey of 480 kilometres did the bus stop for a twenty-minute injira intake, during which I managed to smoke two and a half cigarettes and top up my supply of Game with Marinda cool drinks.

I sent photographs of my wife and children through the bus, and the passengers soon adopted me as their personal firangi. Tsegaye Shiferaw even gave me a pencil with "I love you" printed on it, and the bus driver bought me an ox-tail switch to chase away the flies.

Nothing else happened in the bus, except for an occasional green bag being chucked through the window.

The early start had made me sleepy but I couldn't doze, because every time I nodded off, Hanji would shout to wake me up. I couldn't understand why – perhaps he was worried I would break either my neck or his windscreen as I fell forward.

Then it began to rain. Not just heavily – extremely heavily. At a snail's pace we crawled down dizzying mountain passes, while hailstones smashed into the windscreen like cannon balls.

From what I have told you, it must be clear that I've had no time to miss you – I've been totally focused on staying in one piece.

Now comes the shit part. In pouring rain we stopped here at Dangla for the night. My new friend, Tsegaye, took pity on me. With me in tow, he went in search of accommodation . . .

I am exceedingly brave, as you know, but, my word, the room I was assigned for 40 birr (about R40) is indescribable! I beat the price of the lice-infested, linoleum-carpeted, empty, dilapidated little room without water or linen and coated in seven years' filth down to 20 birr and left my backpack there.

I remained strong – my benefactor meant well and when he left to put down his things, I moved on to the shebeen of the establishment – but, man, it was so bloody dirty that I was afraid to drink even the Bati beer.

Under the diplomatic pretext of searching for a nice restaurant to treat the teacher to a meal, I kept an eye out for better accommodation.

Well, guys, the restaurant was even more syphilitic. I ordered bread and soup. The soup smelt like cow dung and old stable and I swallowed the bread with difficulty. Anxiously Tsegaye asked after my wellbeing.

And right there I sent diplomacy to hell and went in search of a clean place. On the outskirts of the town I found a relatively bearable place at last – a cross between a rundown Masonic in Mara and a dilapidated Royal in Bitterwater.

And that is where I'm writing this despondent letter from.

I wish you were here to share this experience with me. I miss our camaraderie, but I certainly don't wish to be back in the Republic now – after all, the adventure has just begun!

Greetings from one house to another.

Johannes the Traveller

Tuesday, June 21

I slept in fits and starts because I didn't have an alarm clock and no one was going to wake me here in Dangla and I knew I couldn't miss that bus. The rest of the passengers and the driver were sleeping somewhere in town – they couldn't afford my kind of accommodation. After midnight I woke up every fifteen minutes.

It was pitch-dark when I got up. There was no bloody water in the taps of my "expensive" shower and washbasin. I tried to force a bowel movement that wasn't there. Luckily there was nothing in my stomach after last night's camel piss soup. I've acquired a bag of peanuts in the meantime. My diet is going to consist of beer and nuts from now on, because I just can't take the African filth any more. Poverty is all right, but man-made filth fucks me up these days – in my younger days I could live with it, but enough is enough.

True to my nature, I was the first soul at the stop. It was still completely dark outside. Everything was closed, and it was a muddy mess underfoot. Forty-five minutes later Hanji arrived and we unlocked the bus. I loaded my backpack and reserved my seat. While I was smoking furiously, the bus filled up and at six o'clock we finally shook off the mud of Dangla and got going.

Things have changed, I thought, as the driver narrowly missed a cow. In the early years, when you wanted to get away like this, you were truly cut off from the outside world. There was no possibility at all of knowing how the people at home were doing. Or of them knowing where in Africa you were at that moment. But nowadays there are places where you can send or receive an SMS. It ruins my natural equilibrium. Once, when I was in a tight spot, I even began to send everyone farewell messages – for the last time, I thought.

I have always enjoyed travelling alone. There's nothing to restrict your freedom of movement. But being literally the only white man here, I constantly have to remind myself what a privilege and adventure it is. It would be easy to throw in the towel and go home on the first plane. I think I miss my own people more as I'm growing older . . .

In Gonder it was raining cats and dogs. It's the ancient city of King Fasil, where he built the most wonderful medieval castles in 1640. I was here a few weeks ago as well – so the history wasn't important to me. All I wanted now was a bus ticket to Metemma on the Sudanese border, an alarm clock and a tin of Johnson's baby powder for my balls.

I managed to find decent accommodation. I gulped down a Bati or two while writing in my journal. The next moment the gates of the courtyard flew open and, believe it or not, a GP

231

number-plated Nissan Patrol drove up. I nearly jumped out of my skin. My people! I thought and rushed over. I saw the two older gentleman get the fright of their lives as I stepped up – I must have looked very dishevelled.

"Goeiemiddag," I greeted them in Afrikaans.

The driver's eyes lit up.

"Goeiemiddag," he replied in broken Afrikaans – we clearly didn't belong to the same church.

And so I met Enrico Pinto and Mario Tirozzi, unaware of the fact that our lives were going to become inextricably joined in the future.

In English we inquired after one another's wellbeing, the journey that lay behind us and the road ahead. They had been away from home for two months. Enrico and Mario were not what you might call spring chickens – on the time scale, they weighed in on the wrong side of sixty-five. They were realising a dream of many years: to travel from Johannesburg to Italy by road. It was only now that the dream was being realised. They had been too busy making money before.

Enrico, the retired head of Alfa Romeo, South Africa, a former Formula One racing driver with Jacky Ickx in the late sixties, and his faithful friend and confidant, Mario, a technician and Enrico's colleague of many years. Each with a villa in Italy and one in South Africa.

They were travelling in comfort and style. They had everything that opened and shut. Minus 40 fridges, roof tents, satellite phones, GPS, high-lift jacks, gas showers and loads of money.

The long journey was starting to take its toll, however. Their bodies were not handling the (luxurious) discomfort so well. The stretch of road through Northern Kenya had shattered their nerves. They were worried about the situation in Sudan, the war in Darfur, the uprisings in the north-eastern province of Kassala and the rumours that Eritrea was on the point of invading Sudan. What they really wanted to do now was go home. After all, one can enjoy something only up to a point.

Enrico produced a half bottle of vodka and with: "We can't take this over the border to Sudan," he poured each of us a generous shot. After that things just got better. Mario cooked pasta al dente, Enrico bought an extremely shit bottle of Ethiopian red wine and in true Italian style we kept growing fonder of one another. I told them about my ancestor, Rocco Catortzio. Soon we were bosom friends and I had permanent lodgings in Italy.

I even received an invitation to ride in the back of their vehicle with their luggage. Half-drunk, I mercifully declined – it would take the adventure out of my own trip, I argued.

Drunkenly clutching an alarm clock that would hopefully wake me the next morning, I pushed off to my room and packed my rucksack . . .

I am a contract worker in Sudan. I work for a Sudanese con-
struction company in Bahir Dar, Ethiopia. I don't enjoy it. I don't
like Ethiopia and its people. I have been in Bahir Dar for seven
months and I'm on my way home now, to my people in Omdurman, where the White Nile and the Blue Nile meet each other.

I decided to take the money for the plane ticket home, so I'm
travelling to Sudan by bus. I used some of the money to buy
a candlestick for my mother and a box full of clothing for my
younger brothers and sisters.

The way the Ethiopians struggle is too much for me. Their
buses are run down. Everything is difficult. In my country there

are buses with air conditioning and videos. Actually, I already regret not having travelled by plane. Next time. Inshallah.

My family makes clay pots from the mud of the Nile. My father tans and dresses the skins of crocodiles and other animals brought to him by the poachers from the Sud, the swamps of the White Nile in the south of Sudan. My uncles have a nursery on the banks of the Nile. I miss them very much.

I saw the firangi on the bus to Gonder, I even saw photographs of his children. He's a strange man with wild hair and a bushy beard and copper bracelets. He looks crazy. He must be, or why would he be travelling by bus? Surely there are easier ways for a firangi to get from one place to another?

I went to the bus stop early in the morning. There were many people there, but the gates were still closed. Every time a bus drove in or out of the compound, the people trampled one another to get out of its way. These Ethiopians! Then I saw the firangi, head and shoulders above the milling crowd. I saw him fall and disappear under the dark mass. I wondered if he would ever see his people again . . .

At last we all bundled into the bus. If I had thought yesterday's bus was old and run down, then this one was worse. In the front I saw the firangi. Luckily he was still alive. I tried to make my buttock, which was squashed onto a two-person seat with three other people, comfortable for the six-hour journey to the border . . .

Wednesday, June 22

Metemma is nothing but an extended general dealer's store. An incredibly long dirt road with hundreds of cuca shops and stalls, which peddle a bit of everything. I knew I was about to drink my last beer.

Across the border alcohol was taboo. I realised I would need some water too because the guidebooks said there was none to be had in Gallabat, Sudan. Neither was there any public transport to Gedaref, 150 kilometres away. Hitching a lift in a truck was my only hope. As always, I felt vulnerable when I crossed an African border. My heart was in my mouth. To tell the truth, I was shit scared of Sudan.

Totally lost in this remote corner of Ethiopia, I shouldered my backpack and headed for the border post. A multitude of people crowded around me, shouting:

"Hey, you!"

"Hey, mister!"

"Give, give!"

I looked straight ahead and pushed on.

Only six people in the entire bus were going to Sudan. A mother, her two small daughters and her teenage son. Also an open-faced young man, neatly dressed in jeans. When he presented his passport, I saw that he was a Sudanese citizen.

"Can you speak English?" I asked him.

"Yes."

"Boeta, today you must look after me. I'm an old man and I've never been to your country. I need somebody to help me cross this border. I can't speak any Arabic."

And that was how I met Nasser Alladin Abdulah Mohammed. It was providential – an act of Allah.

We approached the Ethiopian customs and excise officials together. My backpack was methodically unpacked – for the first time on leaving a country. I remained friendly and explained about my bracelets. There was a lot of interest in the Ethiopian one and I was given a friendly sendoff. Filled with trepidation at the inevitable bureaucratic shit, I walked out to meet a Sudan of war, hatred, famine, drought and death.

The officials at Immigration were strict. I remained friendly, though there was a hysterical undertone in my feigned laughter. My visa was scrutinised. Perspiring, I completed a form. Then a man demanded 7 500 dinar (US$35) "for registration". I'd forgotten about the "alien registration" procedure and thought for a moment that it was yet another scam. He pointed at a poster on the wall and I understood.

It explained that a stranger had to be registered in Sudan.

The bugger up was that the man didn't want dollars, but dinar, and I didn't have any. He also wanted a passport photo, which I produced from my backpack. My passport was retained, as I stormed out in search of Sudanese dinar. I knew there were no banks in Gallabat. What now? Dishonest black marketeers were standing around with knowing smiles on their faces. I tried to explain. Nasser Alladin was nowhere to be found. The illicit traders just laughed and I knew what was coming. They were going to swindle me without batting an eyelid; I was at their mercy.

I knew the official exchange rate was 250 dinar to a dollar, but no matter how I argued, the scoundrel offered me 230 and refused to exchange anything smaller than US$100. I was snookered, and with a laugh he bamboozled me out of US$12.

I paid my alien tax, received my passport and proceeded to Customs. No problem. The man there didn't have the slightest interest in me or his work. Nasser Alladin was still missing and alone I walked the Sudanese version of the Via Dolorosa. My next checkpoint was Security. Again a photograph and a form. Fortunately no money, and the officials, who could not speak a word of English, were perfectly cordial.

Now everything had been done. I had officially entered Sudan.

In the blinding afternoon sun I looked around me in a daze. Where to now? The next moment Nasser Alladin stood in front of me.

"Come, I organise lift in Boksi."

First, I have to describe a Boksi. It is a two-wheel driven Toyota farm bakkie, usually with a covered steel frame on the back. A Boksi is the long-distance transport of the poor man in Sudan. It is loaded until there is no more room, and then the driver races to his destination across terrible roads as fast as the engine will allow – or so the book says.

Our Boksi was an open bakkie. It was terribly rusty, and there was no tread left on the tyres. The hood was held in place with wire. It was parked with its nose pointing downhill and there were stones in front of the wheels. Next to the bakkie, under a lean-to made of reeds, a group of men were sitting, dressed in white kaftans and sandals, headscarves and kofias. Nasser Alladin and I joined them. The woman of the bus, her two small daughters and teenage son, as well as a great many suitcases were also travelling along and I wondered how the six of us and all our luggage were going to fit into the bakkie.

And then we began to wait. And wait. And wait. And nothing happened, except that the weather changed, and angry clouds gathered. Nasser Alladin got fed up, but to no avail. I was helpless, used to the timelessness of Africa, and I let the nothingness wash over me.

Two hours later I was sitting on the back of the bakkie, together with Mama, children, Nasser Alladin and a shitload of stuff. The children must have eaten something syrupy, for a cloud of flies had descended on them. Those that couldn't find a spot on them, tried to find refuge with me. And still nothing happened. That is not quite true, for every fifteen minutes another soul came along with his luggage and found a place for it on the Boksi. By four in the afternoon sixteen adults, two little girls and everyone's luggage were on the bakkie. Another two got into the cab with the driver.

When the driver finally tried to start the contraption, nothing happened. One of our companions on the back jumped down, undid the wire, opened the hood, fidgeted at the front, kicked away the stones, and we got a "kick start". The vehicle gulped and sputtered, and the driver pumped the gas until blue clouds billowed, then he "crash-geared", I heard the gearbox losing teeth, and we pulled away . . . after only twenty metres the engine died, and I wondered whether I had just been waiting for four hours . . . not to reach Gedaref by that evening. But the man fiddled around some more and we were on our way again. We drove for five hundred metres before stopping at Immigration, where I had been before, and the bakkie's papers were checked and I thought: What for? Another twenty metres ahead Customs and Excise examined all the luggage. The next stop was the police station, where another 50-kg bag of flour was chucked among the passengers on the back.

It's quite impossible to describe how the old bakkie was loaded by this time. All eighteen of us were sitting on top of the luggage, which took up all the space at the back. Most of us had our legs hanging over the side. I was sitting on the opposite side to the driver, and an enormous suitcase was perched between the cab and me, preventing me from seeing the road ahead. Close to me, with their legs also dangling over the side, sat Nasser Alladin and a few of the others. I couldn't see the road behind me either. The two small girls and their mother were seated behind my back, in the middle of the load. Sharp little knees were grinding my alcohol-ruined kidneys to a pulp. On the roof of the cab there was something resembling a chicken coop, loaded with more suitcases.

The driver crash-geared the bakkie into second, then third, and off we sped. Believe it or not, just a kilometre further we were stopped at a military post. My passport was checked. Some of the luggage was opened, cardboard boxes ripped open and with a final: "Where's my mobile, you!" and a finger pointing at yours truly, we were on our way again. The bakkie picked up speed on the horrendous dirt road and we ploughed through dongas, holes and ditches. I had nothing in my line of vision but the bushes sweeping past. Sometimes the vehicle ventured so close to the side of the road that branches scratched my legs. Mercifully there was no feeling left in them, as all circulation had been cut off. When I tried to move my toes, nothing happened at all.

At the next village we were stopped by the military again. My passport was a sought-after item. When I got down from the bakkie, my legs gave way and I fell in a heap in the road. We had been on the road a mere fifteen minutes and Nasser Alladin had warned me that a five-hour journey lay ahead . . .

The discomfort turned into hell, but it was a question of sticking it out. Even if I complained, who would be able to do anything for my salvation? Here I was, somewhere at the back of beyond, all by myself, and if anything happened to me, my family wouldn't even read about it in the papers.

And then, believe it or not, it started to rain. It was as if the heavens opened. It came down in buckets. From the cab, a groundsheet was passed to us on the back. We each grabbed a corner and clung to it for dear life. In the pounding rain, with loose ends flapping, the bakkie sped on through mud, sludge and snot. In my mind's eye I saw myself and the other sorry wretches on the back of the bakkie – and I burst into hysterical laughter.

When the rain subsided, I looked out over an incredibly beautiful landscape. The sun was dwindling above a flat grassland scattered with acacia trees. The fresh smell of wet earth and the clean new life that rain brings made me forget my terrible discomfort for a while.

A constant stream of tankers carrying fuel to Ethiopia came swishing from the front and I could feel how our old bakkie had to focus to stay on the road.

It started to rain again and we drew the groundsheet over us. The little girls behind me didn't say a word, neither did anyone else – we were silent in our suffering. My thoughts turned to other unpleasant days. Travelling by train from Bamako in Mali to Dakar; lying in a snow-covered two-man tent in the Himalayas; bouncing through the Mauritanian Sahara on the back of an open Land Rover; struggling with a backpack through the scree of the Biafo glacier in Pakistan; sleeping on a tarred surface at the bus stop at Meknes, Morocco. And involuntarily I thought of my army days . . . nonstop "buddy PT" during basic training; Vasbyt in the Wolkberg during JLs; muddy bivvies in Sector One Zero; weeks of dry rations in Sector Two Zero; flying in a Puma over Ongiva, Angola, seated among toolboxes; on the back of a Buffel on the cut line in Vamboland.

"You know, I was in the army," I heard beside me. Surprised, I looked at the dazed, dripping figure of Nasser Alladin. "This

240

is exactly how it was. We were never dry, never clean, never had enough food and all the time Sudanese People's Liberation Movement was shooting at us." I took a fresh look at the young man, bouncing along with me on our way to Gedaref. He spoke of suffering, of war, sorrow, fear and despair, and of his country, his people and just how shit it was here on the back of the Boksi in the rain.

Then a suitcase that had been tied to the roof of the cab, came undone and fell on my head. There was no chance of stopping and tying it back on, so I held on to the suitcase, while clinging for dear life to remain on the bakkie.

The next moment the vehicle skidded and went into a spin on the snotty road.

This is it then, it flashed through my mind. The engine stalled and the bakkie didn't roll, but came to a stop with a lurch, the nose pointing back to Gallabat. Now we're completely fucked, I thought. The rain was coming down again and no matter how the mechanic fiddled, it was to no avail. On the back we sat in complete silence, wordlessly contemplating our lot.

It was pitch-dark when the bakkie finally laboured on through the mud . . .

At half past eleven that night we rattled through the streets of Gedaref. Nasser Alladin and I were dropped off at the Amur Hotel. What a dump – shabby, stifling, dusty and rundown. For 4 000 dinar Nasser Alladin and I were given a room with three beds. There was a cold shower. I sprayed the bed for fleas. We went out to drink a Fanta, set the alarm for six o'clock the next morning and went to bed.

What a fucking day!

Mohammed Ahmed Suleiman

At first glance Mohammed Ahmed Suleiman seems dodgy. He looks like a man with a plan. He wears dark glasses. In fact, he is a strict Muslim. But only when he is in Khartoum. There he is a respected man. He supplies seed, agricultural chemicals and fertiliser to the farmers along the Nile. He is over forty and unmarried. He looks after his mother and a number of brothers. His father had two wives. He also looks after the other wife and her children. Two of his older brothers are medical doctors in Saudi Arabia. Occasionally they send a little something back home.

Mohammed speaks fluent English and worked as an interpreter at a hospital in Saudi Arabia for four years. Now he is back.

Someone has to keep the family together. But he dreams of being different, of being free from the daily drudgery of caretaking. That's why he escapes to Addis Ababa for three weeks every year. There he becomes someone else. Where no one knows him, he is simply an anonymous Sudanese businessman. And he drinks wine and takes a pretty girl back to his room every day. He is free from the restrictions that religion, family and work impose on him in Khartoum.

He has a thirst for knowledge, for the world around him. That is why, when he came across a white man from South Africa in a bar in the back streets of Addis, he spontaneously invited him to call on him in Khartoum . . .

Friday, June 24
The city of my youthful dreams was flat, dusty and Sahara brown.

I booked into the Central Hotel, Central Khartoum. At US$27 per night it exceeded my budget, but the place was clean and had a cold shower en suite. After the hellish journey from Addis I felt entitled to spoil myself a little. It was time to get cleaned up properly, wash clothes and regroup.

It was the Muslim Sunday. All the important places were closed for the day. I drank tea in the hotel dining room. My personal opinion was that Health RSA would summarily close down this little eatery. The tablecloths didn't seem to have been washed in the past two years. I learned that breakfast was included in my accommodation.

Good, I thought and sat back happily for . . . two hard-boiled eggs, half an inch of camel cheese, one dry bread roll and a glob of mixed jam. No salt. That was it. But it was paid for and it was safe and I was enjoying my first Sudanese breakfast.

Now I was going to tackle the Nile. With a map of Khartoum, I took to the streets. It was seriously hot when I set off in the direction of the Blue Nile, according to my map. Central Khartoum was dirty. Drains were overflowing and everything was

243

covered with dust, sand and filth. The streets were littered with plastic bags; they were even piled up against the street lights. The taxi rank in the town centre was even worse. It was a continuous stream of rubbish, thousands of decrepit vehicles and crowds of people. But amazingly enough, the people here did not bother me. Though they stared openly at my bracelets and my skin colour, they did not beg for alms. I was not subjected to "Hi, you" or "Hi, mister", as had been the case in Ethiopia.

It was a long walk, but I was fit, and soon I was standing on the banks of the Blue Nile! I was pouring with sweat, but a great happiness settled inside me. I was here, and all that remained now was to see the place where the Blue Nile and the White Nile come together, then I could go home . . . or could I? I took a photo.

Strictly speaking, taking photographs in Sudan is forbidden. The books warn against it, especially in Khartoum. Every second building here belongs to the government, and in Africa it is forbidden to photograph government buildings or bridges. Neither are you supposed to photograph people, for they believe you are interfering with their souls. You're also supposed to obtain a special permit from some department or another – which I didn't have, as it was the Muslim Sunday and everything was closed. But given the day, I believed there would be fewer people on the streets and the government would be sleeping and I'd be able to steal a picture or two.

I turned right to Omdurman and walked to the confluence. By this time it was scorching, and I was pouring with sweat. I walked till I was nearly a goner; in truth, I walked myself right off the map. I was beginning to suffer from serious dehydration. At one stage I walked for six blocks with a Muslim service blaring from speakers in lofty minarets.

At last I reached a massive bridge and witnessed the two large expanses of water flowing into each other. And I took photos! A security guard tried to admonish me, but I was so excited, dehydrated and foolish that I asked him to take a photo of me standing on the bridge. He was so taken aback by the mad white man that he obliged!

I had my photos. I was truly here. A dream of many years was no longer just a dream – it was reality. With renewed vigour I set out on the return journey. I progressed to the Blue Nile yacht club, which today is just a name. No sailing has taken place there for a very long time. The *Malik* lies there, high and dry – the gunboat of Kitchener, the man responsible for throwing our women and children into camps. It was a reminder of 1898, when Kitchener, as commander of the British forces, came to suppress the Mahdist Khalifa and his insurgents and simultaneously to avenge the death of Gordon, the governor of Khartoum. At the battle of Kerari the Maxim machine guns mowed down 10 000 Sudanese warriors, armed with spears and swords. Kitchener's only comment was: "We gave them a good dusting."

I was worried, because I had arranged a rendezvous with my Italian friends, Mario and Enrico, but after four days there was still no sign of them . . .

I headed for the hotel. The sun was setting. When I reached the Al Kabir mosque in central Khartoum, I saw the sun disappear behind a minaret as I looked down the street and, caught up by the beauty of the moment, I shot a photo from the hip, and that was when my own sun went down.

"Come with me," I heard and someone grabbed me by the shoulder. I was on the point of getting angry, but when I turned . . . a policeman.

"You took a photo?"

"Yes, of the mosque," I answered. I looked round and, believe it or not, I was standing next to a fucking police station. Now I was truly buggered, I realised immediately. I mustn't lose the unlawful photographs of the confluence, I thought. The man dragged me to the charge office. It is the shittiest thing that can happen to any traveller: an African interrogation and jail. I felt paralysed with fear. My arse was tightly pinched, like a tobacco pouch, and my brain had stopped dead. I had no plan up my sleeve.

They hustled me into an office. There were six uniforms, sporting a variety of insignia.

"Why did you take the photograph?"

"Where are you from?"

"Where is your permit?"

"What are you doing in Khartoum?"

And I explained. I explained that I was from South Africa, that I was a personal friend of Nelson Mandela's, that I had travelled 8 000 kilometres just to see Khartoum, that I had had a dream, that I had played goalkeeper for Bafana Bafana and that I had a friend in Khartoum and his name was Mohammed Ahmed Suleiman and that they could phone him . . .

And Mohammed Ahmed Suleiman came to fetch me and my camera with the photos of the bridge where the Blue Nile and the White Nile come together, and we went out for a kebab with onions and he took me from one place to another in his town, and he asked about South Africa, and when at last I said goodbye, he asked me if I would send him a magazine. Especially one with photos of Zulu women doing a traditional dance.

And I realised: Tits saved my arse today . . .

I was flying across the Sahara, following the coastline. I was bitterly disappointed – glad to be out of Nouadhibou, but sorry that I had been unable to cross the Sahara overland. I was slightly irritated and I was taking it out on poor Ferdi . . .

Sunday, September 24 (eight years before)

In a month's time I would be forty-one and what a forty-one-year period it had been! An incredibly blessed life about which I had not a moment's regret. Materially I might not have collected much, but my coffers were filled to overflowing with adventures, experiences and mental treasures.

Ferdi and I had no idea where in Nouadhibou, in the northwest of Mauritania on the Moroccan border, we found ourselves. We were too afraid to show our faces in the streets, where Islamic children would pelt us with stones. We were waiting to be smuggled out of Mauritania to Morocco.

The house in which we were had no windows and the only sunlight fell through a ventilation hatch in the flat roof. We lay on the tiled floor and read, slept and drank coffee. The uncertainty of whether we were going to leave at all, and if so, when, made the wait even more unsettling. Worst of all, Magmud, the smuggler, had disappeared. It had been forty-eight hours since we last saw him. We had no idea what the status quo was.

To while away the time, my old mate of many journeys and I played a game with coins on the tiled floor. I finished my only book; we made soup; I smoked an entire packet of cigarettes. Would we be leaving, or was this the end of our Saharan crusade?

After an 8 000-kilometre journey from Abidjan in the Ivory Coast, hitching rides and using public transport, we were stranded. The Nomadic inhabitants of the southwestern Moroccan desert were insisting on an independent state, Western Sahara. Their spearhead was the Polisario Front that had become embroiled in a guerilla war. Mauritania, acting on an agreement with Morocco regarding certain territories, had initially resisted the Polisario, but their only railway line had subsequently been blown up, which had brought the export of iron ore to a halt. Furthermore, the border region between the two countries was littered with landmines. Mauritania had withdrawn from the battle and only Morocco was still vehemently opposing secession, though a United Nations cease-fire was in operation in anticipation of a referendum. Internationally the Polisario had wide support, and even South Africa acknowledged Western Sahara as an autonomous state of the Polisario.

Because of the danger of landmines and the fact that three French tourists had been blown up eight months before, Mauritania had closed its border post. Morocco, yielding to foreign pressure, had kept its border open. Convoys smuggling vehicles and luxury items arrived from France on a weekly basis and disappeared into Mauritania and Senegal.

Traffic was still moving from north to south, let through by the Moroccans. A convoy then found itself in no-man's-land, surrounded by landmines, and faced by a closed Mauritanian border post, which actually had no choice but to let them through. No traffic from south to north passed through the official Mauritanian post, therefore anyone travelling in that direction had to be smuggled through the minefields to the Moroccan post by way of a detour. After that, clearing had to be obtained from Rabat to move through the military zone to Dakla, 350 km to the north.

And now we were waiting to be smuggled through the landmines . . .

It was three o'clock in the afternoon when we shook off the dust of Nouadhibou's streets, bouncing on the back of a fucked up open Land Rover. The wheels were rolling and Ferdi and I laughed like naughty children who had just escaped from detention. A great adventure lay ahead. The vehicle made for the mouth of the Cap Blanc Peninsula. To exit the peninsula, we had to pass through a police post, a customs post and finally a military post. These posts restricted movement into and out of Nouadhibou. These were the people who had to be bribed by the smugglers. The official border post and military posts between Morocco and Mauritania some distance ahead had to be strictly avoided.

There were six of us on the back of the Land Rover: Ferdi and I, two Moroccans and two Mauritanians. We were sitting on top of the luggage. The advantage of this, I told myself, was that the luggage would absorb part of the shock if we detonated a landmine and we would be flung out of the vehicle. In front, with Magmud Mohammed, sat a surly kaftan-swaddled woman and her husband. He looked like a Touareg, with his Ninja headdress allowing only his eyes to show.

It was incredible. Nouadhibou refused to let go, for scarcely had we passed through all the posts when we had a bloody flat tyre! The only spare wheel, suspect and battered in appearance, was taken from the back. The two of us, who would ordinarily have volunteered for the job, left the desert dwellers to muddle on themselves. At R750 a head for the trip, some sardines and bread . . . what had we expected anyway?

The two passengers in the front seemed a pain in the arse. The woman sat at a distance, giving orders. The Ninja tried to tell us that the way we had been sitting at the back had caused the flat tyre!

And Ferdi lost it completely. Using a mixture of Afrikaans and English, my soft-spoken friend tried to tell the Ninja not to tell him, Ferdi, who had travelled for miles through much shittier regions, that it was his fault that the vehicle had had a flat tyre!

Ferdi is big and dark, with a bushy moustache. He stepped closer and raised those banana hands and the Ninja, who hadn't understood a single word, nearly jumped right out of his rags. He stumbled four paces back and I suddenly feared the long knives were going to come out and Daddy was going to meet an unsung death somewhere in the dunes of Mauritania. But with his tail between his legs, the Ninja sat down behind his wife, who was still shouting orders about how the wheel should be changed.

At last we struggled on. Magmud was battling. He couldn't find the gears. I feared we were going to get stuck right there, and the sand was not even thick. Suddenly we stopped. The sun was still high. We were confused. Had the vehicle broken down? In broken English Magmud explained: "No, we're sleeping here tonight, and tomorrow we'll move through the mines to the Moroccan border post in the dark." Could that be so that the Mauritanians would not see us?

A groundsheet was spread and the desert dwellers made tea. Ferdi, knowing that there was only one spare wheel, began to repair the flat one. I found us a place that was sheltered from the wind. Believe it or not, the woman tried to motion to me that I should help pump the wheel. I sent her to hell in silence.

The wind came up and sand soon filtered in everywhere. We put on our own Ninja headdresses, but the sand penetrated everywhere: nose, eyes and arsehole. Then, suddenly, the entire Mauritanian contingent disappeared into the twilight without a word and left us two infidels alone in the Saharan night. (We learned later that a railway man had a shack nearby and our fellow travellers had gone there to seek shelter.)

We made coffee on our primus, ate bread, sardines and sand and crawled under the covers. We huddled close together. Sand heaped up over us.

Covered by cloths and braving the wind and sand, Ferdi, in a serious mood, spoke of the time when he was a sapper and lay waiting to go in and blow up the Tanzam railway line in Zambia. My old friend didn't often speak about his war experiences but I knew he had suffered damage. One day he would tell me, but in the meantime I knew, regardless of what tomorrow might bring, this heap of sand next to me was the best heap I could possibly wish for as a companion on this hellish journey.

The day of the "border run" arrived. We had loaded our stuff, and were having coffee when the children of the desert returned. They were in a hurry, but we took our time to finish.

When the sun stuck out its head, we were already speeding along through a stark desert landscape. We raced up one dune and down the next, bouncing and jostling, hanging on for dear life.

Then Magmud suddenly turned left and made a dash for the railway line in the distance. Now we were really bouncing. The railway line was about two metres higher than ground level and we were approaching it at full speed. The bliksem didn't slow down at all, and we took to the air and flew across the tracks. When we hit the ground, the rigging of the Land Rover, to which we had been clinging, gave way. I was nearly catapulted over the hood, but the man sped on. The jolting was painful and almost unbearable, but at least the wheels kept turning in the right direction.

We finally came to a stop at the foot of a high dune in the valley. I presumed we were out of sight of the Mauritanian military posts and found ourselves in no-man's-land. Now Magmud had to show his mettle, for this was landmine country.

The old Land Rover struggled through the thick sand. Magmud still couldn't find the gears and we were in danger of getting stuck. Then it happened, and we had to get down and push the vehicle out. While we were driving, I kept a lookout for old tracks ahead of us. At least one other vehicle had passed here, so we were reasonably safe, unless delayed-action mines were used. Now and then Magmud went his own way. I didn't know where the landmines were, but I hoped and prayed that he did.

On the horizon we saw the Moroccan machine gun emplacements and we knew we had reached the most dangerous part of our journey. There was no conversation in the back of the shuddering vehicle. We held on and hoped the nightmare journey would end soon. The wreckage of blown-up vehicles was scattered everywhere. Suddenly we came across piles of stones that were obviously meant as markers indicating a road. If we deviated from it, we would be blown to smithereens.

The Land Rover could no longer negotiate the high dunes. We often had to push and lay down sand ladders. Ferdi and I remained in the compacted vehicle tracks. While I was pushing, drenched with a cold sweat, I glanced up at the dug-in Moroccan soldiers. From their vantage point at the top of the dune they were probably enjoying the sight of the poor sods in the green Land Rover painfully struggling along in the valley below.

After a four-hour struggle, we reached the boom of the military border post, 300 metres outside Morocco – so near and yet so far!

Nothing happened. There was no movement inside or outside the military fort situated about 900 metres away. Nestling against a dune, the fort was equipped with embrasures, barbed wire and cannons.

After about half an hour six soldiers and a corporal appeared, all armed with shovels. What now? They walked down the side of the dune to the road ahead of us and began to remove the sand. No one even glanced at the green Land Rover and its dazed occupants.

Some time later a solitary figure came walking towards us from the direction of the fort. It was a neatly dressed, burly lieutenant. He spoke French and collected everyone's passports. Ferdi and I didn't say a word. He scrutinised the passports of all the natives. When he laid eyes on our passports, he looked up for the first time. He studied them carefully and looked at us again. I realised I had to try everything and wordlessly handed him the letters that Unisa and our embassy in Dakar had written in French. In faultless English he asked us to wait and disappeared into the fort. Things didn't look good.

Forty-five minutes later the man put in an appearance again. With military precision he explained the situation. No African passport holders were allowed to pass through this border post, with the exception of Mauritanians (who might have relatives in Western Sahara). It was a war zone under the control of the military and the diplomatic situation was irrelevant. Moreover, South Africa acknowledged the enemy regime.

The explanation was sincere, and I realised that he wasn't looking for a bribe but was just executing orders. It would be no use arguing with him, and he certainly did not care about Mandela. I saw sympathy in his eyes, but he remained inflexible.

The upshot was that the South Africans had to turn back, but the desert dwellers would be allowed through. Magmud was in two minds, but he realised we would have to turn back. Everyone was dismayed – it was back through the minefields again. As we drove away, I realised my dream of crossing the Sahara had been shattered at a distance of a mere 300 metres. In the cab the woman was chattering like a machine gun. I couldn't understand what she was saying, but it was clear that she was very unhappy; as a matter of fact, it sounded as if she was shitting on the driver's head.

The next moment the vehicle came to a stop. Magmud ordered us out in the middle of the minefield and told us to pitch camp and wait for the next convoy from north to south. You're crazy, I thought to myself. We refused to budge and I could see Magmud was desperate and close to tears. He felt responsible for us but he also felt bad about the Mauritanians who had to go back.

We continued on our journey to Nouadhibou. The place was like an octopus. It wouldn't let go; its tentacles reeled us in time and again.

The woman in the front was incensed and had such a tiff with Magmud that he lost his way in the middle of the minefield, completely missing the markers. We only became aware of it when the passenger door flew open in transit and the woman and the clever Ninja tumbled headlong out of the Land Rover. Bread and sardines scattered across the sand. The vehicle did not stop, but the passengers in front had decided they'd be damned if they were going to be blown skyhigh along with it.

I shouted at Ferdi to stand up, because it would give us a better chance of surviving the shock of a landmine explosion. The Land Rover was now struggling along off the beaten track. I was gripped by immense fear. I looked at Ferdi and saw bewilderment in his eyes. Then, to add insult to injury, the bloody vehicle got stuck! We jumped down and began to push – landmines, my arse. While we were pushing, I looked up and barely ten metres ahead I saw the wreckage of two other vehicles that had been blown up.

It was with a huge sigh of relief and a feeling of gratitude that we found ourselves back on track. The passengers who had jumped ship came walking towards us, stepping carefully in our tracks. The swaddled woman looked ashen around the eyes.

We were heading back towards the railway line. I realised that the driver was in deep shit. The Mauritanian army, who had still been tangled in their bedclothes early this morning, were up now and the desert was open. It was important for him to get back on the Nouakchott/Nouadhibou main route, or he would be facing a jail sentence. So would we.

Again we flew through the air over the railway line, and sped on at breakneck speed. And believe it or not, we got stuck again! Magmud's eyes were wild. I could see he was close to breaking point and was going to burst into tears at any moment. He shouted: "Pusti-pusti, quick, quick!" We did our best, reacting to the urgency in his voice.

At last we reached the coastal road. Our nerves were shattered, as was the vehicle. We stopped and Magmud opened the hood – the Land Rover had overheated. While we were waiting for it to cool down, I saw him scan the surrounding dunes worriedly. A large tear rolled down his cheek and I knew something was terribly wrong.

We had scarcely progressed another 800 metres, when a sand-camouflaged desert vehicle with three camouflaged Ninjas inside came out slowly from behind a dune. Now we're completely fucked, I thought, and in my mind's eye I saw us spending the rest of our leave in a Mauritanian jail.

Our passports were collected wordlessly by a one-pip lieutenant. He walked back to his desert crab, with Magmud following in his wake. We couldn't hear a thing. Even if we had been able to hear, we wouldn't have understood. A long conversation and emotional explanations transpired and at last Magmud returned. He was pale, but he had our passports. Without a word he gave them back, got into the vehicle and drove on.

AND NOW?

And now? Had I done everything that I had set out to do? All the travelling had left me completely wasted. Totally kaput. The loneliness and filth were getting to me. Shouldn't I just go home now? I could simply get on a plane and in a flash I would be home . . .

After all, I could always go to Cairo later. Why struggle through the Sahara now and possibly not even reach it? It had been more than a month and a half since I left home; wasn't it time to turn around?

The Sahara? Was it my last chance? I had previously tried but not succeeded. Would I get an opportunity again? Was it now or never?

This was a train I didn't want to miss! The trans-Sahara from Khartoum to Wadi Halfa. Two hours before departure I sat sweating in the shabby waiting room of Khartoum North. The book said the railroad had been built by Kitchener in 1898 to transport his troops and provisions from Egypt to Khartoum. The book also said the journey was supposed to take 36 hours, but a good average was 46! That was because sand regularly blew over the tracks and the train had to be dug out . . .

There was a horde of Sudanese and Egyptians on their way north. I waited patiently. This was one thing I managed to do only in Africa: wait. I had learned here that it was no use getting excited. In South Africa and other Western countries you *had* to lose your temper to make things go more smoothly – here it did not work.

Then the train puffed into the station. It was grey: painted grey, and grey with dirt. Everything looked old and run down. The people pushed forward. I was carried along by the surging crowd. My train ticket, first class, was in Arabic, as were the numbers on the carriages. I tried to compare the markings on my ticket with the number on each carriage, but it was an impossible task. A railway man in a grey uniform came to my rescue and steered my luggage and me onto the train.

My first-class passage entitled me to a place in compartment three in the third carriage from the front, which had six upright seats and a few tiny luggage compartments overhead. This was no SAR&H sleeper. The sole difference between first and second class in any African train is that in second class at least eight people are crammed into a compartment.

I was first and chose a window seat with my back to the locomotive. I knew about the shit, soot, smoke and dust that would be blowing in at the window.

One by one my fellow travellers arrived, stowed their luggage and sat down. And thus began one of the most interesting journeys of my life.

My fellow passengers conversed as if they had known one another for years, but everything took place in Arabic. As far as I was concerned, it might as well have been Greek; I didn't understand a word. That is not quite true, because I had learned three words in Arabic. It is said that Sudan is ruled by IBM – not the computer giant, but the following three words:

Inshallah – "God willing"

Bokara – "Perhaps tomorrow"

Malesh – "I'm sorry".

In other words, "Malesh bokara Inshallah" could be said to mean "Sorry, I don't have a fucking clue."

Opposite me sat Montasser Haroun Saleh Hassan. He was

thirty-nine years old and dapper in dark glasses. He worked for a travel agency in Aswan. His mother was Sudanese and he was returning from a ten-day visit to his uncles and aunts in Khartoum. He had a hearty laugh; his teeth were worn away and brown from smoking. His broken English was my only line of communication with the rest of the passengers.

Next to him sat Saleh Mohammed, a friendly young man from Wadi Halfa. He understood a smattering of English, was presently studying at the University of Khartoum and was on his way home for the holidays.

Then there was Assad Abdul Mohammed, who looked a bit like one of Ali Baba's forty thieves. A smooth Egyptian smuggler. He was loud and bombastic and immediately took charge of our compartment. It all happened in Arabic, though, so I took no notice. He was about fifty and from Suez. He often travelled back and forth on this train to attend to his business interests in Egypt and Sudan.

Beside me sat a quiet young man with large, sad eyes and a permanently pained expression on his face. He seemed well-to-do. His clothes were neat and new, he had a gold chain around the neck and a Walkman on his ears. Maaz Mohammed Abdrogman didn't say much, and spoke only Arabic. He understood no English at all. He was a TV technician on his way to a two-week installation contract somewhere in Egypt.

At the door on my side sat a thin, dark, bearded man. His beard was long, his eyes dark and sinister. He was traditionally clad in a white Sudanese kaftan and turban. He said nothing; didn't even offer his name. I had no idea what he did, or where he was going. Behind his back, the other passengers had christened him Osama bin Laden.

The resemblance to photographs I had seen, as well as the fact that Sudan had offered asylum to this dreaded terrorist and enemy number one of the Western world made me wonder . . .

Slowly the train steamed out of the station. It was stifling already as we moved through the suburbs of Khartoum. The

Arabs around me chattered incessantly, Assad most of all. He spoke loudly and gesticulated wildly. Opposite me Montasser just smiled and indicated that the man was talking shit. I smiled quietly in my own corner.

It became even hotter and, as predicted, diesel fumes and dust blew in at the window. Every traveller had a little parcel with food and water. Wordlessly Maaz offered me a doughnut-like cake. Saleh stuffed one cigarette after another into my mouth. Here people shared, I realised, and produced my bag of peanuts. The men helped themselves. My Ethiopian Nyala cigarettes weren't popular, however. We continued on our journey along the banks of the Nile.

To the left lay the mighty river in all its glory and to the right a barren desert of rock and sand. There was so much water, but the green belt stretched barely 200 metres along the banks. I became aware that the train was carrying more passengers than those seated inside. There were also hangers-on and people on top. Crowds of young boys sat on the roof or hung between the carriages. I wondered how they were able to endure the scorching sun.

The train steamed into Shendi. During the Middle Ages it was the trade mecca of Sudan, centrally situated, where the caravan routes from West Africa converged with the routes along the banks of the Nile. Here wares from Venice and India used to be bartered for gold, leather, wood, horses and camels, but the most profitable business of all was the traffic in people. A premium was put on young girls and castrated young men. It is said that some slave traders allowed potential buyers to try out the young girls for three days "on approval" before selling them, which, of course, was nothing but prostitution.

But people get what they deserve, and today Shendi is an insignificant dusty dump.

Montasser and I got out and I bought a bag of ice. The water I had brought was warm and I hoped the ice would help cool it down. There was no way I was going to put the suspect ice into the water, however – I planned to place my water bottles on top of it. In the end all I managed to do was create wet, muddy sludge on the floor of our compartment. No one complained – and I realised that these people were incredibly tolerant of one another, even inside a confined space like this one. Everyone had their shoes off by now and if a man wanted to rest his feet on the opposite seat, the people on that side made room.

Only thirty kilometres to the north we passed the antique pyramids of Meroë, the ancient Kushitic capital, dating from the third century before Christ. They stood lined up on a sandy ridge, resembling those in Egypt, but miles removed from tourist crowds, camel touts and belly dancers. I had heard that the cursive Meroëtic writing had still not been deciphered by archaeologists.

The landscape visible from the train did not offer a lot of variety. To the left were the banks of the Nile, covered with palm and date trees, and to the right, rocks and low, flat houses. The train made regular stops between nothing and nowhere, during which the engine driver and his colleagues crowded around one of the wheels of the carriage in front of us – something was clearly wrong. Ahead lay a 500-kilometre journey through the Sahara and a breakdown would result in a massive rescue operation.

It was dusk by the time we crawled into Atbara, the Sudanese version of De Aar. We would be taking in diesel and were scheduled to stop for two hours. This is where the Nile welcomes its last tributary, the Atbara, which rises in the Ethiopian highlands, at Mekele with its salt caravans.

Wordlessly, Maaz and I had tea in the souk. It was stifling, and, even if we were able to, we would probably not have wanted to speak. Just sitting together was enough. Some time later, as Montasser and I were lying on the hot platform, the railway workers unhooked the carriage in front of ours and shunted another one into place. The two-hour stopover became three. Our estimated 36-hour journey had already been delayed by six hours, but Wadi Halfa was beckoning, Inshallah.

Just as we were preparing for the night, the train came to yet another stop. I got out. It seemed the men were not happy with the "new" carriage up ahead either. We were about 30 kilometres out of Atbara. Opposite me in the dark stood a lone mosque on the Saharan plain, the moon a thin sickle beside the minaret. I lit my pipe, lay down on a warm dune and watched the conference under the carriage. After a great deal of jabbering and gesticulating, the engine driver got back into his engine, the conductor blew his whistle and I jumped back onto the train.

I stood in the open door as the wheels jerked into motion. Then, wham! An enormous bang set sparks flying, and the engine and the first two carriages uncoupled and disappeared into the dark. There I was, abandoned along with the rest of the train in the bare, open Sahara, shouting: "Hey, wait for us!" Nobody heard.

I thought: This is how it's going to be then, my trans-Saharan effort thwarted yet again. If I missed the Wadi Halfa ferry, I'd have to go back . . . I surrendered to my destiny.

Before long, however, the engine and its two carriages came reversing out of the dark. The conference began anew. Now there were about fifteen officials, gesticulating, talking, shouting and grumbling. Booklets that looked like manuals were produced. Two-way radios crackled, and I realised this was major shit.

Assad joined me on my dune. I understood from his gestures that the "engineers of Atbara are on their way". After a while a Land Cruiser came speeding along the track. A lot of welding, swearing, bustling and tapping took place. I thought I even noticed some galvanised wire, but at last the two carriages were reconnected.

The train eventually departed late that night, and the passengers could finally settle down. Maaz and Assad spread their prayer mats in the corridor. Saleh spread his mother's sheets at our feet and lay down. Montasser had the opposite seat. I half-reclined, with my legs above Saleh's head and my feet next to

Montasser's. Osama in his white robes lay curled up like a foetus on the two seats next to me.

It was with a sigh that I put my Walkman on my ears and with Karq-Elert's "Nun danket alle Got" and the warm Saharan wind rushing through the window, I said thank you for the enormous blessing that the train was moving . . .

Tuesday, June 28

When day broke I felt gritty. We were still on the banks of the Nile and would be turning away only at Abu Hamad, heading straight across the Sahara from there. The train moved at a snail's pace and sometimes even more slowly, where the tracks were buried in the sand.

Assad was vociferously organising the entire compartment again. He indicated that he would be treating us to a traditional lunch at Abu Hamed, but first we all had to take a bath in the Nile. If I perish, I perish, I thought. I'm not afraid of Nile crocodiles, but, fuck, this man drank train water, so what were we going to eat?

After the night's sleep the occupants of our compartment had developed a firm bond. We all trooped the hundred metres to the river and amid loud laughter everyone, with the exception of Osama, washed in the dirty water of the Nile. I looked at my fellow travellers: Maaz with the pained expression, cheerful young Saleh, neat and finicky Montasser and loud, bombastic Assad, and I realised I had grown to love them.

With us in tow, Assad went looking for somewhere to eat. We filed into a filthy, stinking place. Nasty! I could imagine how horrified the people at home would be. Assad went into the kitchen himself, cut up onions and brought out a huge bowl of fuhl and a few flat loaves. He dumped the loaves among the flies, old food and sticky mess on the table. And everyone dug in – they tore at the bread and dipped and plunged it into the lentil soup, licked their fingers and dipped it into the communal bowl of smirrie again. Even Osama joined in heartily, without saying a word.

Again I thought, if I perish, I perish. I had been constipated for three days and if I didn't get the runs after this, then my guts were probably tied in a knot.

Afterwards we had a tea session, barefoot, on prayer mats under the trees. I noticed that every stranger stopped to stare at me and ask "What on earth . . . and those bracelets?" My fellow passengers thoroughly enjoyed the attention and explained enthusiastically. I belonged to them, and they were looking after me.

The train whistled and we continued on our journey. Now we were travelling across the hard Sahara – gravel plains as far as the eye could see and an occasional inselberg towering into the sky. I was in my element: at last I was crossing the Sahara – that is, if the train didn't break down, Inshallah!

We stopped at station number 10 – in the middle of nowhere. I asked Montasser to take a picture of me against the darkening desert. Then we sped on. I was on a total high.

At station 6 the staff served us with fuhl and bread. Tonight Osama was paying. We sat sweltering under a corrugated iron lean-to and cheerfully shared our meal – we were the A-team, the occupants of *the* compartment in the train. Our fellow passengers fussed around us, but we closed ranks. The Sahara was beautiful. And Johannes Bakkes, dirty, tired and white, became an Arab . . .

The men settled down for the night, but tonight I stood in the open door, looking out over the moonlit Sahara. I was listening to my Walkman. Mike Batt's "The Ride to Agadir" echoed in my ears and there was a cigarette in my mouth. The warm wind blew through my soul. I prayed and said thank you. I hung out of the train – I was euphoric! In front of me the dunes of the Sahara swept past and I was transported by a moment that is impossible to describe.

Wadi Halfa is a desperate place. A place like that should not exist, but it does, for it's the ordinary person's thoroughfare to Egypt. It was once on the banks of the Nile, but when the Aswan dam was built in 1963, the town disappeared. The people resettled about five kilometres from the shore, but their energy had been drowned along with the town. Today Wadi Halfa is no more than a border post offering two boarding houses and other cheap lodgings for weary travellers. The border bureaucrats are as desperate as the town. They compensate for being fed up and frustrated by making it as difficult as possible for the helpless traveller to leave Sudan.

The ferry leaves Wadi Halfa every Wednesday. That gives you one chance per week. If you miss it, you are stranded. It must be terrible to remain in Wadi Halfa for longer than a day.

At three in the morning we jolted to a halt at the station. A few scattered lights revealed the location of Wadi Halfa about a kilometre away. There was only one car at the station. A black one, or so it appeared in the dark. Three kaftaned figures whisked Osama away in the car. The rest of us set out for the village on foot, carrying our luggage. During the journey an incredibly firm bond had developed between strangers and strange ones.

Assad took control again and organised accommodation. We were allocated five beds arranged in a square among forty other already sleeping travellers. I sprayed my dirty mattress and Montasser's and lay down fully dressed. Before long I was in dreamland. I dreamed of fleas, lice, cockroaches, rats and mosquitoes.

When I woke up, it was already sweltering – though it was not yet seven. I was thoroughly filthy, but mercifully had not contracted gyppo guts. There was the smallest hint of it, but when I saw the ablution hole, everything involuntarily clenched shut.

I washed my face, arms and feet in a bucket and felt somewhat less gritty.

I was afraid of today's red tape. Assad wanted to take charge of everything for Montasser, Maaz and me. Saleh had gone somewhere to see his mother. An agent demanded our passports and 7 000 dinar. My book said the total for checking out of the country should not exceed 3 000 dinar, and I was unwilling to relinquish my passport. In a strange country your passport and your personality are *all* you have. Without your passport you are nothing. Through Montasser, I let Assad know I would embark on this excursion myself, even if no one understood me. I picked up my belongings and walked down the dusty streets of Wadi Halfa.

According to the book, a great deal of administration needed to be done before you could board a ferry to Egypt:

•The ticket bought in Khartoum had to be authenticated at a ticket office here.

- Dinner tickets for the boat were sold at another hatch for 800 dinar. A ticket was compulsory, or you couldn't go through Immigration.
- Harbour tax of 1 800 dinar had to be paid at the shipping office.
- The Health officials had to check your yellow fever inoculation, and if they weren't satisfied, they would inoculate you on the spot.
- If you were a stranger, you had to report to the police, who would validate your strangers' stamp and give you a slip of paper.
- This you took to Customs and Excise, where they would make an entry in a register after they had collected your slip and received your payment of 200 dinar.
- At Immigration two forms were obtained and completed; one you returned to Immigration, the other was stamped and handed over at the harbour. This was unofficially accompanied by a baksheesh of 500 dinar, passed under the table.
- You then loaded your luggage into a Boksi and rushed over to the terminal building, three kilometres away.
- On arriving there, you waited for hours for Passport Control to put in an appearance. Then you hurriedly handed over your stamped form from Immigration and got your passport stamped.
- At the terminal, Custom officials pulled everything out of your backpack and slapped a blue sticker on your bag – indicating that everything was in order.
- Then you boarded a rickety bus, loaded to capacity, that took you a further two kilometres to the quay.
- When you arrived at the boat, your ticket was scrutinised and your passport taken.
- Passportless, you got on board and settled in among 600 other souls in the hold below deck and hoped you would see daylight and your passport again some day.

"Johan, is that you?" I looked around me, bewildered. Who the hell knew me in this place?

And there on the porch of the police station was Mario Tirozzi, the South-African Italian I had met in Gonder. He seemed to have aged overnight; dazed, unshaven and shrunken, he was flanked by two constables. On his face was an expression of dismal despair.

He rushed over and he fell around my neck.

"I've got big problems," he whispered in my ear as the police stepped nearer.

"Where is Enrico?" I asked. And the story was revealed. They had arrived here three days ago. To transport their vehicle across the Aswan dam, a separate ferry had to be hired. This boat didn't take passengers, only the vehicle and its driver. Enrico and the vehicle had left the day before. It was then that the bureaucratic doors had closed for poor Mario. He had been too late for a place on today's ferry – they refused point-blank to give him passage. He had already spent two hundred American dollars in bribe money, which had disappeared into the streets of Wadi Halfa together with the person who had taken the bribe. He had no money left; his spirit was broken; he was close to tears. I looked at the bewildered old man and suddenly he reminded me of my father. Amid my own uncertainty, I told him not to worry, things would work out. I assured him there was no problem big enough for me to leave him in this dump. He just had to wait there for me.

I set out in the heat, uncertain of where to go first. I asked around. My Arabic was shocking and the English of the townspeople even worse. At last I was directed to a queue. I fell in line. It moved frightfully slowly. It seemed that the town mafia got preferential treatment, for they arrived with stacks of passports of people who had paid them commission and pushed to the front. I couldn't afford to throw a tantrum and decided to wait patiently in the sun until my turn eventually came.

Assad, Montasser and Maaz appeared – they had decided not

to leave me alone – and fell in line with me. Now things happened more quickly. Assad shouted and shat upon every official, and in a jiffy our tickets for the boat were certified. Through Montasser, I explained Mario's problem to Assad.

With Mario tagging along, we returned to the ticket office, but no matter how Assad threatened and scolded, Mario would have to spend another week in this dump, and I, as a man of my word, would have to stay with him. I was overcome by despair. No matter how I tried to rationalise, there was no way I was going to leave the old man here on his own.

We set out for our next destination. At the lower end of the street we noticed a black car – a Mercedes with dark, tinted windows. Leaning against the vehicle were three white-kaftaned, robed men with automatic pistols. Osama emerged from a government building with more bodyguards in dark glasses. I had a feeling and stepped closer, dragging Montasser and Mario along. The guards wanted to step in, but Osama stopped them and Montasser explained. The black car disappeared with Mario inside . . .

With this rigmarole over, we sat down to eat Nile perch – stacks of flat fish, deep fried and served on newsprint. They looked awful, but by now I was used to everything and I tucked in with gusto. The four of us ate and the fishbones piled up. I had grown very fond of these men. They had treasured me like gold. Despite having divergent personalities and being hampered by a lack of communication, we understood each other perfectly.

Then the black Mercedes swept up. Smiling broadly, Mario got out. The tinted rear window was rolled down halfway and with a slight nod and a wave Osama disappeared. "Now you stay with us." And the men of compartment three in the third carriage of the trans-Sahara train took the Italian under their wing . . .

At dusk we found ourselves on the deck of the ferry, on our way to Egypt. The Colossus of Ramses II changed colour in the setting sun. I had spread my jacket and a sleeping bag under the lifeboat for Mario. He was completely done in. Montasser and I lay on my groundsheet. From his bag he produced a small joint of Khartoum hashish. We puffed at it contentedly – though I realised I was looking for trouble. Not being an habitual user, I was bound to fall overboard if the stuff made me get up and walk, but the moment had called for it and the A-team would look after me.

A crash boat came tearing through the swells. Armed to the teeth, the boat moored onto the ferry. Loud announcements came over the speakers. Montasser swallowed the joint.

"What now?" I asked.

"Don't know, but they said everybody should stay with their luggage and not move."

Half an hour passed before a man in a white robe was respectfully helped into the crash boat, and so Osama bin Laden disappeared from my life.

I hadn't washed for four days. My balls were stuck to my legs. My hair was caked with dust. I was booked into the Noohan Hotel somewhere at the back of the busy souk in Aswan. The small room was sparse but clean. I threw down my backpack. Getting clean was not my first priority, however – it had been ten days since I'd tossed a cold beer down my gullet, and without delay I made my way to the bar of the small establishment. Here in Egypt they also drank on the sly, as in Morocco. In other words, if you wanted to drink, then you did it furtively, somewhere at the back. It was the start of my relationship with Stella, Egypt's prime beer. I immediately threw back two 500-millilitre bottles.

It was like nectar. Could anyone have it so good, I wondered, and realised again that a bit of suffering lent a new dimension to the ordinary.

Armed with a handful of washing powder, I jumped into the shower at last and washed and washed and washed. Everything except my only pair of pants. Luxuriously I stretched out on the clean bed of my thirty-rand room, and watched the ceiling fan revolve. I was dog-tired but so bloody glad to have shaken off the dust of Sudan. Now only Cairo lay ahead, and then I could go home . . .

I had unpacked my backpack. All the cloths, jewellery and souvenirs I had bought in Ethiopia and Sudan were on display, draped all over the room. I sprayed my bed, hung my Addis shirt over the headboard and this back room somewhere in Aswan became my own.

But lazing around is something this Bakkes has never been able to do. I put on my wet T-shirt and my dirty pants and went in search of a clean pair, driven by the luxury of my surroundings. I wanted to buy some deodorant too; I'd run out in Addis Ababa already.

It was noon and the Arabian market was teeming. Startled, I realised there were other Westerners too! Fat, pale ones in shorts and flip-flops, scorched pink by the sun and shabby in appearance.

Damn, I'm glad I'm not one of them, I thought, and wished them gone. This was *my* trip, who were these cast-offs from an aeroplane, sauntering around, buying banana-leaf papyrus and plastic pyramids?

My walk through the souk turned into a game. The Simien mountains walking stick and bracelets drew a lot of attention. Everyone wanted to touch and feel, and to know where I came from.

"Janoob ifreeqiyaa" called forth "Nelson Mandela" and "Bafana Bafana". "Ali Baba," they said, referring to my beard, or "Rambo," referring to the bandana. I heard:

"Welcome in Egypt."

"Welcome in Aswan."

"Welcome in Alaska" (a humorous reference to the heat).

"Come into my store."

"Looking is free."

"I'll pay you to have a look."

"Do you want tea?"

And so I had to defend my wickets and my money. Egypt has only shit for sale and I knew these fellows were going to take me for a ride if I didn't take care. The minute you showed interest, they were all over you. But I wanted a pair of pants. The Arabian "pantaloons" didn't work for me, but Mustafa claimed that he had just the thing for me. I was made to sit and handed some mint tea. His window display had nothing to my taste, however. I gesticulated wildly.

"No problem," he said and offered me a cigarette. Then he disappeared for a while and came back with something in navy-blue that resembled tracksuit pants, neatly embroidered with "Nike". I grinned at the blatant rip-off.

I realised that the pants would work for me, but Mustafa's opening bid of 180 Egyptian pounds (almost R200) nearly made me choke in my tea.

"Don't quote Nubien prices! What's your best African price?" I snapped, offering 80 pounds. The grief and suffering on his face and the protestation that he himself had paid 150 pounds for the pants made me laugh.

I took my time sipping the tea. I lit another cigarette, offered Mustafa one and spoke about the poverty in South Africa. "Ninety pounds – my last price," I said and pretended to get up.

"My friend, my friend! Please, nothing less that 120. You're killing me," Mustafa lamented.

"Mustafa, everyone must make a living and I don't want your children to be hungry. I'll be generous, but no more than 100 pounds. I can't offer you more, otherwise I can't go home to *my* children." I got up to leave.

"I'll accept 110. My poor children!" He threw his hands into the air.

"Sorry, but a hundred was my last offer," I said and walked away.

About a hundred metres down the street Mustafa and I sealed the deal at 100 Egyptian pounds. A good transaction for both of us.

That evening I had a tryst with Stella . . .

I found her very beautiful. The balmy air played with the chiffon scarf that was draped nonchalantly over her hair. When I arrived at the roof garden of the Nefertiti Hotel in Luxor, where I was staying, my eye caught hers and she smiled archly. Then she fixed her attention again on her companions. She was deep in conversation with three young Egyptian men, each an Adonis in his own right.

I was searching for a guide to accompany me to the Valley of the Kings. Actually I had no desire to see pharaohs' graves, mummies, pyramids and sphinxes. A Stella beer and a belly dance in Cairo were all I was still interested in before I returned home, but while I was here . . .

Apart from the pretty girl, the company consisted of men only. Two were playing pool. A few others were enjoying coffee and a bubbling pipe. I asked, but there was no Stella.

I made further enquiries. Yes, Ahmed at the pool table can take me. He's a tour guide. I watched the game and now and then my eyes locked with those of the girl. I wondered whether she recognised the danger of the game she was playing, alone among a crowd of Egyptian men? Many Egyptians see Western women as an opportunity to test the water, without repercussions and the stress that Muslim traditions place on extramarital relationships. They believe Western women are "easy", and it can land the unsuspecting female traveller in a very unpleasant situation. I had been told of felucca skippers who hung their "tackle" over the side of the boat, hoping that the length of it would make the women weak in the knees.

Ahmed approached me. Yes, he would take me to all the sights on the western bank of Luxor tomorrow. Included were a number of temples, a variety of holes harbouring mummies, a whole lot of statues and an alabaster factory. A full R200 for the whole shebang, transport included. Expensive, I thought, not included in my modest budget, but I was here, after all . . .

"Let's play a game of pool; if you lose, you give me 10% discount; if you win, I'll add 10%," I proposed.

And when I looked up from the cue, I saw the woman look at me and I looked back. Then, with a last meaningful glance, I left the roof garden with the next day's excursion clinched at R180.

Now it was Stella and I. In the garden restaurant of the Luxor Hotel I found myself a table. After a few shots I imagined I was Mark Antony and the girl from the roof garden was Cleopatra. All I needed now was a bronze goblet, a bunch of grapes, a handful of dates, Cleopatra herself and an adder.

It was dark by the time I took to the streets of the souk, searching for my bronze goblet. And sure enough, I found a beautiful one – antique and tarnished green, but solid in my hand. Now to test it with a cold Stella, I thought as I headed back to the restaurant.

"Leave me alone, please! That's enough! You're hurting me!" I heard from a dark alley. I caught a brief glimpse of the roof garden Cleopatra. The Adonis confronting her was smaller than I. Stella, Simien mountains walking stick, bronze goblet and I approached menacingly.

"I wondered what had happened to you. Our table at the Luxor Hotel is ready. Come," I said, taking her hand and leading her into the light.

When we were seated at my restaurant table, I ordered a Stella each for Cleopatra and me. The dates and grapes were forgotten.

"Thanks," she said and I looked at the beautiful woman. She didn't seem overly traumatised. My girls – mother, wife and daughter – would have been slightly more upset after an experience like that, I thought.

276

"Where are you from, what are you doing here so on your own?" I asked in my flawed English.

"I'm from Denmark and a student of the Arabic language. I decided I need to practise by speaking to the people," she answered in English with a Danish accent. I asked our waiter, Ahmed (in Luxor everyone is called Ahmed), for Aquavit. He brought more Stella. And we talked about travelling, about the people at home, about Scandinavia and South Africa and Egyptian rapists and border wars.

"I lied to you," she told me.

"About what?" I asked, somewhat surprised, wondering whether she had forgotten to tell me about the poison and the snakes.

"I'm not a student. I *am* studying Arabic but I'm a sergeant in the Danish military intelligence. They are sending me to Iraq to trace and interpret Arabic radio messages. I need to understand the people so that I can safeguard our soldiers who are part of the peace-keeping forces over there."

And the Stella reminded me of the words of Ronnie Price of Ronnie's Sex Shop, somewhere on route 62: "Fighting for peace is like screwing for virginity."

"I'm a soldier and I can look after myself, but earlier today when I saw you, to me you looked like Eric the Viking and I couldn't keep my eyes off you."

And the sergeant fluttered those long lashes . . .

Needless to say, that night in the Nefertiti Hotel it was a bronze goblet, a snake and I . . .

No dates and no grapes. And Cleopatra . . .?

My Western viewpoint has led me to the conclusion: Muslim women have a hard time. I realise that I don't understand the culture; their outlook and logic are a mystery to me. My acquaintance with women in Dubai, Pakistan, Mauritania, Morocco, Sudan and now in Egypt was zero. They were simply not there – at any rate, you didn't see them. And I believe woman is the crown of *my* God's creation. But let me put that aside for the moment.

Friends Koos and Anna had been to Egypt.

"If you do get to Egypt, you *must* call on Noha. She was our guide. We flew her out to Paarl for a visit. She's a wonderful person, a strict Muslim, but with a thirst for knowledge and new experiences."

When I made enquiries in Luxor, however, I learned that Noha was on leave, visiting her parents in El Minya. And that was where fate stuck its hand into my pocket again. In the early nineties the Islamic disapproval of Mubarak's relations with Israel boiled over. Especially in El Minya. Tourists were abducted and murdered. The situation was so bad that, even today, no tourist will visit the place. Embassies and guidebooks advise against it.

Fuck them, I'm going, I thought, rising to the occasion.

Tuesday, July 5

This morning I had a good-sized hangover on board – exacerbated by the fact that last night's engagement with Stella had made me lose my head – with dates, I mean. I had taken my malaria medication a day early. Larium has always had the effect on me of stuffing up my quality of life for half a day.

Apart from aches, self-pity was also a factor.

I don't enjoy travelling on my own as much as before, I thought. I wish Nanna was here. It's unbelievable how a woman can make one's life easier. She would immediately have taken over the admin: buying the train tickets, boarding the train, finding a seat, getting off at the right place, and all without any of the tension usually associated with organised travel. That wife of mine has a knack of taking charge, and the older I get, the more I struggle with the usual shit that accompanies the ordering of my affairs. How can one possibly marginalise women? I wondered.

The anxiety of not knowing where to get off began to weigh me down. As always, everything and everyone was Arabic – signs at the train station, conductors and fellow passengers. During the entire six-hour trip I sat ready to jump off at a moment's notice. I had memorised the Arabic scribbles for El Minya, but the train didn't stop long enough at the stations. If I took the time to compare the sign with my memorised squiggles and scrawls, I would have only a few seconds to get off. And all this for a woman! the hangover protested.

Eventually I found myself on a windswept platform, baggage and all.

⚱𓀀𓃒𓀀⚱ said the sign. "El Minya?" I asked a passer-by, pointing at the sign. He gave a little laugh and pointed at the station building. "El Minya, yes," he replied. Pointing at the sign, he said, "Tooiaaleet."

Well, accommodation was my first priority, and after that, Noha. Cairo was waiting, and this was just a brief interlude en route to my ultimate goal. The *Lonely Planet* travel guide, acquired in Luxor, advised against a visit to El Minya, but recommended the Palace Hotel to stubborn, hard-boiled, indigent travellers, and that was what I was searching for as I walked down the street. In the foyer there was an enormous painting of Nefertiti. Like Cleopatra and Tutankamen, this girl represents the ordinary guy's idea of Egypt. Oh, and add to that the Rosetta Stone, as illustrated in my standard six history textbook.

But what do we really know about Nefertiti? Her name means "the beautiful woman is on her way". She must have been beautiful. She was the wife of Pharaoh Akhenaton, who lived in the mid-1300s BC. The Sun God was his deity of choice – the direct antithesis of the traditional gods of the time. Egyptologists believe that Nefertiti influenced him in that respect. The breathtaking "unfinished head of Nefertiti" can be seen as part of the Armana Collection in the Cairo museum, or so the guidebooks say. It depicts her as ravishing, but in other likenesses she resembles her husband, Akhenaton. Were women denied a presence in history even then? She might have outsmarted them in the end, however, because some historians believe that she ascended the throne after her husband's death under the name Smenkhkare, and reigned as pharaoh for a short while. And all that we have of her today is a bust in a Berlin museum. Nefertiti the beautiful. I wondered about Noha.

For forty Egyptian pounds I booked in at the hotel. The foyer was packed with uniforms: policemen, railway policemen, traffic policemen, soldiers and metro policemen! As soon as I walked in, the walkie-talkies began to buzz.

I needed money, so I put my luggage in my room and enquired from the hotelier where I could exchange dollars. As I headed for the door, a furore erupted, with the combined forces protesting loudly. Radios chattered. The hotelier barked in Arabic and a designated member of the forces grabbed me by the arm and dragged me up the street. It dawned on me that it could result in an international scandal if I was abducted. For that reason they were not going to let me out of their sight!

Once I was in possession of the right currency, my bodyguard wanted to return to the hotel, but a new place must be explored on foot, it's the only way to get a feel for it, and I decided: To hell, my friend, if you want to be my escort, you'll have to keep up with me. And I walked. I walked until that the corporal must have longed for the days of his basic training.

Back at the hotel at last, I explained to the hotelier that I wanted to go for a walk along the Nile. I also explained that I didn't have to be looked after. I was nearly 50, had just come out of Sudan on foot, knew Cleopatra personally, had been a soldier myself and was just a tiny bit afraid of my wife . . .

A long argument ensued on the radio and I was subsequently left in peace. Perhaps my former bodyguard had convinced his commander it would be to El Minya's advantage if extremists traded me for Saddam Hussein.

I phoned Noha and regretted it immediately. There was an uneasy tone in her voice. She didn't seem keen. It was probably only for Koos and Anna's sake that she ended up agreeing to meet me at my hotel that night.

What a surprise El Minya turned out to be! The Nile is at its most beautiful there, more beautiful than in any other place, and it was just the inhabitants of El Minya and I. They were friendly and asked a lot of questions. A felucca sailed past, there were beautiful gardens, young people were strolling, children played

soccer, the smell of cooking was everywhere. A perfect calm settled over the place, while the setting sun turned the world a different colour. There were no tourists, and therefore no bustle.

I dressed up for Noha. That is to say, I took a shower and tried
to get my hair under control, for I had nothing smarter than my
Aswan Nike pants and a clean T-shirt for the occasion.

As I was walking down to the foyer, there was a power cut.
The hotelier offered me a seat outside on the pavement. I thought
about Noha and realised that it was taboo for an unmarried
Muslim girl to meet a strange man in the street. But it was too
late for tears. I watched the cars flash past. El Minya was busy.
People were flocking to the Nile. Even if I had known what Noha
looked like, there was no way I would have recognised her in this
bustling crowd – cloaked and veiled or not.

A fully cloaked woman with a pink shopping bag was making a
beeline for me. A suicide bomber, I thought anxiously. Sad eyes
and mouth.

"I'm Noha," she said and I was at a loss for words. I shook
her hand before realising that that, too, was unacceptable.

"Thank you for coming. Is there a place where we can drink
coffee or tea? I won't keep you long, but Anna and Koos were
adamant for me to meet you," I said.

She avoided my eyes and nodded.

"Wait," she said and went across to talk to my host and the
armed forces that were lurking in the dark somewhere behind
me.

Around the corner was a neat little restaurant. Again she spoke
earnestly to the staff and management before we were shown to
a table.

The circumstances were entirely unnatural. Because I had never been good at handling embarrassment, I rattled on about my
trip, conveyed greetings from South Africa, commented on the
beauty of her city, all of this in two minutes. Silence . . .

"I can't stay long, my sisters are visiting from Kuwait," she said and presented me with gifts for her friends in Paarl. Even a piece of jewellery for my wife.

Silence . . .

I looked at the young woman in front of me. I couldn't tell whether she was pretty or not. I didn't know what her hair looked like. Was she slender or plump? I saw only liquid brown eyes and a generous mouth.

Then I *wanted* to know. Not what she *looked* like, but what she *was* like.

"Yes, it was not easy for me to meet you, that's why I had to explain to the men at your hotel and over here that I'm a tour guide and you're a client. This is a business meeting."

She was thirty years old. Yes, her parents had arranged two marriages for her, but she had had the right to refuse, though she wasn't able to choose the man, no, they didn't understand about marrying "for love", her work was everything to her, but when she got married, she would have to stop – then her sole obligation would be to look after her husband, children and household, the wide world would then be closed to her, no, it didn't bother her – it was tradition, but her visit to South Africa was possibly the highlight of her life, yes, she would very much like to experience other parts of the world, but it was actually impossible for a woman, even if she was a tour guide, her parents put a lot of pressure on her, all her sisters older and younger were already married, she would probably not be able to refuse again, a cousin had just asked for her hand and it looked as if her parents were going to agree, she didn't really know him, but he would be a good husband . . . And while she was telling me all this, her eyes were telling a different story.

When I walked her to her taxi across the dark street, I was afraid to take her arm, as I was accustomed.

And as I was accustomed, the world lay wide open for me – tomorrow I was going to Cairo.

The paraffin wick is burning high. He sits hunched over the table. The magnifying glass moves slowly across the inscription. For
months he has been staring obsessively at this piece of stone. Can
that be the problem? He has been looking at it for too long. He
sits back, wipes the sweat from his brow. Lost in thought, he lights
his pipe. He looks again at the Greek inscription – that he under-
stands, but what do these pictures say? My word, he's so tired . . .

The traveller stoops through the darkened doorway. In the dark
alley outside, the men smoking their bubbling sheesha pipes
pointed the way with meaningful glances. It is July 26, and long

past the midnight hour in Saharia, in the slum district of Cairo. The long knives are out. Here you walk like someone on a mission, because without a mission you're going to be relieved of your knackers, that's for sure.

The room is thick with hashish clouds. Umm Kolthum, Egypt's Piaf, is crooning a melancholy tune. Call-girl red lips are pouting, the traveller is met with a jingling embrace.

"Buy me a drink," a provocative voice murmurs, "and I'll show you a thousand and one Arabian nights . . ."

"Jean-Francois, come to bed now! It's late, you'll never understand what it means," a shrill voice calls from downstairs.

"In a minute," he mumbles and slowly moves the magnifying glass across the stone.

Why couldn't Napoleon's soldiers have built their damned fort in a different place? Myopically he cleans his glasses.

Thank you, Ptolemy Epiphanes, for trying to remove our debt, for wanting to repair our irrigation system and for wanting to eradicate hooliganism, it says in Greek. And the pictures?

The traveller settles into a corner and orders a Stella beer.

"What about me?" A supple Nefertiti spreads her arms wide. This is Cairo's dark side. Overpowering smells, deafening music, surging, stirring, shady, sweaty figures. "Only a mummy would be able to resist tonight," the traveller grins.

"This damned piece of basaltic stone," Jean-Francois Champollion sighs and his thoughts go back to how this stone ended up lying here in front of him on this day in the good year 1822. The deceased emperor Napoleon Bonaparte invaded Egypt in 1798, hoping to undermine Britain's access to India. For three years his troops dug themselves in. His soldiers built a fort. Fort Julian, where the western arm of the Nile worms its way through the delta and flows into the Mediterranean Sea. The piece of basalt became visible in the sand, and someone must have understood

Greek, for on the stone were an inscription in Greek and these indecipherable pictures. Then the English came in possession of the stone, and the thing lay in a British museum, and the English gave it their best shot, and now, after twenty-one years of fruitless efforts to decipher the stone, it is finally lying in front of a Frenchman again.

A breast is shamelessly displayed, the laugh is defiant, the second Stella is halfway, the mummies are waking up.

"There's a wife and children at home," Tutankamen says, and the hashish grins.

"If you only see one belly dance in your life, it had better be in downtown Cairo," she says. And Red Riding Hood, the call girl, smiles broadly at the wolf.

Thank you for tax relief, exemption of military service and thank you for this resolution of yours, Ptolemy, carved out in solid rock. Thank you on behalf of the priests of Memphis, Jean-Francois Champollion reads. "Damn, I am reading the pictures!" he says out loud.

And unaware that the Nile eventually spends itself at Rosetta on the Mediterranean and that the Rosetta Stone on display somewhere in a London museum was deciphered by a Frenchman in 1822, the traveller drowns with Dante, Faust, Lucifer and the belly dancers of the dissolute Palmyra dance hall.

Thursday, July 7

Today was the day I was going to make arrangements to go home. I had ticked off Cairo. It was time for an Ethiopian visa and air ticket. Early in the morning I walked the eleven kilometres to the Ethiopian embassy and, chop chop, I was in possession of a return visa; now there was only the ticket to arrange, then a beer with Pottie, friend and military envoy in Addis, and Daddy would be going home. High time.

The offices of Ethiopia Airways and Egypt Airways had not yet opened. There was time on my hands and ha! Right there was the Egyptian museum!

Fuck, there were droves of tourists, as there were at any Egyptian tourist attraction (and there are many). And it's not even breakfast time, I thought. The groups were about thirty strong, and each had a guide with a flag. The guide led the way, chattering in Chinese, Taiwanese, Mandarin, Mongolian, spouting an endless stream of shit about mummies, statues and stone caskets, and the wide-eyed and slit-eyed tourists responded by saying "eh" and "heh", and everyone was happy, and I wished I was back in the south – where they don't feed you shit; they just shoot you and *take* your shit.

There is a circle route through the museum, and, just to be different, I went against the flow. And suddenly I found myself alone among a mass of people, all pushing in the opposite direction, following the flags. A different world was opening up in front of me. I was being carried away by a past and a history that forced me to a stop. No one had ever told me this – and we, with 350 years behind us, think we know!

The magnificence of a civilisation that existed so many years before our own Western ingenuity astonished me. Like a zombie I stumbled through the exit at last. On a pillar a photocopied A4 notice proclaimed: *The Rosetta Stone.* With an arrow pointing to the outside of the building. Ha-ha, I remembered from my standard six history textbook, the thing is in England nowadays.

In the blinding light I lit my pipe. Now to get my air ticket and go home. Sheet of A4-paper on a pillar and an arrow pointing around the building. *The Rosetta Stone!* I remembered the small photograph of the black stone, standard six history, chapter one.

And I walked around the building – to a deserted parking lot. Not a soul in sight. A mobile television unit with wires and cables was parked alongside the building, about 200 metres away. And I approached . . .

Then a wheelchair ramp leading to an entrance in the basement of the building.

"Hey! Hey, you! Come back! You're not allowed! No tourist! Come back!" I heard the sound of running feet behind me and I realised there was going to be shit, and I charged down the ramp and I pushed open the glass door and I came face to face with the picture of 37 years ago. The Rosetta Stone, in a glass case, and before the security guards manhandled me roughly back up the ramp, I saw what Champollion had stared at for years, before Egyptian hieroglyphics had fallen into place for modern man, and I knew: Fuck the air ticket, I had to see Rosetta, where the Blue Nile spills its blood into the Mediterranean for Europe.

Saturday, July 9

I got up filthy and in a foul mood. I hadn't slept well. Something had bitten me last night. Actually I'd lost the inclination and I certainly didn't have the energy to arrange transport from Alexandria to Rashid via the back roads. Rashid is the Arabian name for Rosetta. It is a distance of about 160 kilometres but it is off the tourist routes – I had covered thousands of kilometres by now, but organising this trip felt like an insurmountable obstacle. On the other hand, giving up now would be like turning back 200 metres before you reach the peak of Everest . . .

I got into one taxi after another, all empty at first but filling up rapidly, and so I proceeded deeper into the delta. No one spoke English. I simply said "Rashid", and someone would take me by the hand and lead me to the next stop. The drivers seemed to be going nowhere at such a speed that I was afraid we might actually find the place. And then at last, Rashid . . .

I walked down the street, past old buildings and fishmongers. Fish and prawns fresh from the Nile and the sea! Then the Rosetta Nile lay in front of me in all its magnificence. Now there was only the estuary, and it would all be over. Not a soul spoke English, but I understood that the river mouth was some distance out of town. I hailed a taxi.

The man understood bugger all. I pointed at the Nile, made waves with my hands and pointed to the left. Still he did not understand. I dragged him to a chemist's shop – perhaps a more educated man would understand. Even if he didn't understand Afrikaans, at least he'd be able to understand English. But alas . . . Fortunately he did understand my gestures, and the taximan and I agreed on a fare to take me to the mouth of the Nile.

And it seemed as if it was meant to be that way, because our taxi was a peacock blue 1924 Chrysler or Plymouth, and the driver looked like an older version of Antonio Banderas, and I felt like Lucy Jordan on my last drive, and we drove through an unmanned boom, and in front of me lay the Mediterranean Sea, and I saw Africa, my continent, offering to my ancestors in Europe a piece of fresh water from its belly.

As I was taking my coupe de grâce photographs, Antonio and I were apprehended by a platoon of soldiers, who told us that this was a military zone and no fucker with or without a camera was allowed here. And as they bundled me into a police van, I thought: Fuck you, even if you throw me in jail now, you can't take anything away from me. Not you – no one! My dream has become reality! And smiling broadly, I sat myself down and I laughed, for in my hand I was holding a thick Cuban cigar while I sipped contentedly at a tall glass of sparkling wine from my own country . . .

When the traveller stopped at the mouth of the Rosetta Nile, he saw a group of Egyptian soldiers bundling a laughing tourist into the back of a police van. The traveller shook his head and caught the boat to Gallipoli on the Turkish coast. Calcutta was waiting . . .

BIBLIOGRAPHY:

Briggs, P. *Guide to Ethiopia*, 2nd ed. Bradt Publications, UK.

Clammer, P. *Sudan, the Bradt Travel Guide*, 1st ed. Bradt Travel Guides Ltd, UK.

Humphreys, A. et al. *Egypt Lonely Planet 2004*. Lonely Planet Publications Pty Ltd.

This is where I draw the line

"Guys, I'm stopping here, I can't and I won't go any further," I panted as I sank to the ground next to my comrades. We were climbing Ras Dashen, the highest peak in Ethiopia and at 4 500 metres the fourth highest peak in Africa. It had been a murderous three-day hike through mountains and valleys, sometimes climbing as high as 4 200 metres and then descending as low as 2 800 metres. I couldn't go on.

When do you call it a day? I have never done anything by halves. I have always done everything with commitment and passion. When I play, I play hard; when I work, I don't rest. When I wore a uniform, I was a dedicated soldier; when I played rugby, I ended up in hospital. When I take a drink, I do it properly – to the chagrin of my loved ones – but when I go on the wagon each February (admittedly the shortest month) I apply my mind to that as well.

Four of us were doing a "crash course" in Ethiopia. Before our guides and muleteers had led us into the high Simien mountains, we did the rounds among the Coptic monasteries and bars of Bahir Dar and the medieval castles and hotels of Gonder. There were no brakes. "You're like a guy who revs a car so that it's permanently in the red," remarked Roland, my personal ophthalmologist.

I know, I thought, and carried on regardless, knowing that the mountains lay ahead, and that this battered old body was going to suffer. But I had done it before, and I pushed aside the painful thought of the physical suffering that was just around the corner.

At Sankabar in the mountains all our equipment was loaded, and we trooped behind our guide along the Simien escarpment. The views and panoramas were incredible. I realised once more what a privilege it is to have the means and strength to be able to experience such adventure. It was not easy, mind you. Above 3 000 metres my smoke-riddled lungs began to rattle. The carousing of the previous few days – or was it years? – poured from my body. I thought wryly of a previous instance in the

Naukluft mountains when I had suffered so badly that I had promised Kalie that I was never going to smoke again and would jog every morning on my return. He had just laughed. He knows me well.

Dog-tired that first evening, we poured a gin and Game and sat down in style for a meal prepared by our Ethiopian attendants. We didn't last long that night, but went to our tents, each with his own thoughts. It is usually at those times, tired, lying in my sleeping bag, that my thoughts turn to my family at home, so distant and unattainable . . .

My lifestyle and my restless spirit had them at their wits' end. My wife was tired of looking after me. Cara, my daughter, was terrified that I would die. Marc secretly hoped that his dad would change, but I just blundered on.

After an early breakfast we continued with the ascent. Eventually we reached 4 000 metres. It was high, and the lack of oxygen left me completely drained. My three friends seemed to walk effortlessly. I am two years their senior, but surely that couldn't make so much difference? It was somewhat demoralising to see them breeze along ahead of me, but it was my own fault, and I couldn't complain. In the mist on the mountain our tracker and I spotted the rare Simien wolf. It was so remarkable that I put my arms around the fellow's waist and spun him around excitedly. Ethiopia, its mountains, its wolf and its Danakil desert had been a dream for years. My exhaustion was temporarily forgotten.

Throwing in the towel is not quite within my frame of reference.

If you take something on, you finish it, it went through my head the next day as we reached a saddle at 4 200 metres and began the descent to the valley where Ambikwa lay – the base camp for the ascent of Ras Dashen. It had literally taken every ounce of strength to get to the top. I was stumbling along in a daze. Spots danced in front of my eyes, my arm felt paralysed and suddenly I feared my nearly fifty-year-old ticker would give up the ghost. I remembered Cara's words of farewell: "Pa, please come back in one piece."

When do you say: "This is where I draw the line"? I also knew that my mind was stronger than my body and that I would walk until I dropped in my tracks before I would call it a day.

"Pa, please come back in one piece."

My backpacking comrades of many years knew that I wasn't very good on the uphill and that my forte is flat country and downhill, but this sheer precipice was terrifying. It was 1 200 metres, nearly perpendicular, and if I had understood correctly, we would have to come back this way again the day after tomorrow. I was overcome by despair. At this rate I would be left behind to spend the rest of my life as a mad lay preacher, bringing the good news to the people of the Ambikwa valley, I thought cynically.

I was between the devil and the deep blue sea. Should I spend tomorrow resting for the return journey, or should I climb Ras Dashen and then – totally knackered – try to tackle this hellish staircase to heaven again? I couldn't expect my comrades to drag me up here either.

Was it time? For a quieter life? For the comfort of suburbia? Was it time to change my lifestyle? To change my personality and contemplate suicide of the soul . . .?

The next morning I was up and ready, boots and all, but it was here, at 3 600 metres, that I bade my mates farewell. It was hard. As they moved higher up in the dim light of early morning, I felt the urge to get to my feet and stumble after them. Instead, I took out my pipe, stuffed it and drew on it appreciatively. And while the Simien mountains changed their colour to a purplish red, I knew you don't ever say: "This is where I draw the line."

You just regroup for the next day.

An after-story

I've had a truly wonderful innings. Hit a few sixes, and also a few decent fours. Scrambled through here and there for a single, while the scoreboard kept ticking over. There were a few anxious moments, a dropped catch here and there, a few occasions when I was almost run out or stumped . . . but I always managed to come back with another fine drive through the covers.

Perhaps there'll be one last six over the grandstand. But if I get bowled out now, or perhaps run out in the confusion, I wouldn't hesitate. I'd walk towards the Great Changing Room.

I would raise my bat in tribute to my teammates and wave at the spectators.

Glossary

Amakosi (pl.) – chiefs or rulers; singular form – "Inkosi"
Askari – Arabic for "soldier"

bakkie – a small open truck; a pickup
baster – person of mixed race; half-breed
bivvies – bivouacs; temporary camps under little or no shelter
bliksem – an exclamation expressing frustration or anger; or a
  vagabond/bugger
Boer – hist. a Dutch or Afrikaans-speaking inhabitant of southern
  Africa; a Dutch or Afrikaans-speaking soldier fighting against
  the British forces, especially during the Anglo-Boer Wars
boetie – little brother; an affectionate form of address to a young
  male relative or friend
Bonnies – popular name for Bonne Espérance, a dry red or white
  house wine made by the KWV in Paarl
braai – to barbecue (meat, etc.)
Buffel – an armoured, mine-proofed troop-carrier used by the
  South African Defence Forces
bywoner – a tenant farmer who works another farmer's land in
  exchange for the right to work part of the land for himself

civvy – civilian
cuca shop – a small shop selling beer and other things like
  biscuits, candles and sweets

dagha – building mortar used for laying bricks and for plastering
  walls and floors
donga – a dry gully or watercourse that has been eroded by
  running water

dolos – an animal knucklebone or carved object that is used by traditional healers to foretell the future

dominee – a minister of the Dutch Reformed Church

Dopper – member of the Reformed Church

duwweltjie – an indigenous plant which bears small, thorny seed pods

fynbos – a type of vegetation consisting mainly of small trees and shrubs with fine, hard leaves, characteristic of the Western Cape

garrie – popular name for a Land Rover

geloof – faith, belief

gyppo guts – diarrhoea

hardekool – leadwood

impi – an armed band of African fighters; an African tribal army or regiment

induna – a headman or councillor in traditional Nguni society

jakkalspisbossie – *Zygophyllum* sp.

jirre (Here) – Lord

JLs – Junior Leadership course

joiner – a Boer who fought with the British forces during the Anglo-Boer South African War; a collaborator

Khaki – Boer name for a British soldier

kikoi – a coloured cotton cloth worn like a sarong around waist or hips

kleinboet – little brother

knopkierie – a short thick stick with a knob used as a weapon

koeksister – twisted or plaited dough, deep-fried and dipped into cold syrup

koppie – a prominent hill or peak

lobola – payment of goods, cattle, or money by an African
bridegroom to a parent or guardian of his bride

mahobohobo – small to medium-sized evergreen tree, *Uapaca
sansibarica*
matjieshuis – a mat or rush hut
meneer – sir
moer of a – helluva; tremendous

Nama – an African ethnic group of South Africa, Namibia and
Botswana
neef – a nephew; a male cousin; a form of address from an older
to a younger man
Ndebele – a nation of people of Nguni origin who live in South
Africa and Zimbabwe

oom – uncle; a term or form of address for an older man
Oorlams – a group of people of mixed Khoi and Cape Dutch
(Boer) origin, who migrated into Namibia from south of the
Orange River
Ossewa Brandwag – a cultural paramilitary and political
organisation promoting Afrikaner nationalism during and
after the Second World War
ouboet – older brother; affectionate form of address for relative
or friend
ouma – grandmother
oupa – grandfather

pampelmoes – an alcoholic beverage made from a large citrus
fruit resembling a grapefruit
Piet Cronjé – a general in the Boer forces during the Anglo-Boer
Wars
platteland – country districts, rural areas
pop – a doll; a shop dummy

sangoma – a traditional healer or diviner

smirrie – a slapdash stew

Statebijbel – the Dutch authorised version of the Bible

Strandloper – a member of the Stone Age communities of Khoisan fisher-gatherers living formerly in the Western Cape

Suidwes-lied – the unofficial national anthem of Namibia (formerly South West Africa)

SWAPO – South West Africa People's Organisation, a former liberation movement in Namibia, currently the ruling political party

swarthaak – *Acacia mellifera; Acacia retinens*

tannie – auntie; a polite way of addressing an older woman

trekker – a person who treks, often a pioneer

Tukkies – the University of Pretoria

vaaljapie – a rough new wine

Vasbyt – a tortuous route march undertaken by members of the South African Defence Force with full kit and minimum rations

veldskoen – a rough suede ankleboot or shoe, usually with a light rubber sole

Volla – the abbreviated name for a Volkswagen Beetle car

Witboois – a subgroup of the Nama people, led by the Witbooi family. Chief Hendrik Witbooi (1825-1905) is probably its best known member.

Acknowledgments

Photographers:
Nanna Bakkes
Cas Bakkes
Margaret Bakkes
Cara Bakkes
Kalie Kirsten
Johann van der Merwe
Danne Berglund
Lindie Myburgh
Marek Patzer
Ina Burger
Nicol Stassen
Johan de Kock
Elmine Berry
Roland Berry
Ferdi Barnardt
Security guard, Khartoum
Taxi drivers/passers-by/bystanders/drinking cronies/general
public/yours truly

– Rita Britz, who initiated the translation process by making a
lot of good suggestions over a bottle of wine
– Joey Smith, who, with extreme patience, attempted to type an
illegible handwriting
– Etienne Bloemhof, who kept pestering me with the words:
"Just stop travelling for a short while and write something."

But for someone who has lost his Muse, travelling is easier.

303